Love in Five Acts

A Study of the Song of Solomon

Marvin McKenzie

I have, for years, been interested in preaching and teaching through the Song of Solomon but, until recently, was hindered for one reason or another. I recently finished teaching a series of lessons in the adult Sunday school of the wonderful church I am blessed to pastor in Puyallup, WA. It is now my pleasure to present to you those notes, modified only slightly into this book form.

I chose to teach through the Song of Solomon from the point of view that the majority of preachers used until more recently. This book will view the Song of Solomon as a lesson concerning Christ's love for the believers. We will not attempt to find a spiritual application for the more sensitive passages. Instead we will see them from a broader of intense and intimate love for the Lord.

You might also find it unusual that we will view Solomon himself as the villain of the plot and not the hero.

Should you find the book is helpful to you, or if you have questions, that you feel free to contact me.

My e-mail address is marvinmckenzie@bbcpuyallup.org.

To my church,

Dearly beloved of Bible Baptist Church in Puyallup, WA. You have been patient and kind to me for all of these years. I consider myself to be blessed beyond measure to be a servant of the Lord beside you.

There is no such thing as a perfect church and certainly we are not perfect. I do see us as a sound church, a Scriptural church and a solid church.

Thank you for your kindness and devotion to me and my family.

Index

Section One - Introductory lessons

Chapter 1

SOLOMON'S BEST
Song of Solomon 1:1

Years ago my family and I took a vacation to Yellowstone National Park. I took along a book called *The History of Preaching* by John Broadus to read while on the trip. Broadus writes of a preacher by the name of Bernard of St Claire and says that during his lifetime he preached no less than eighty six sermons out of Song of Solomon and had just barely begun the third chapter when he died. That amazed me. How, I thought, could a preacher find that much preaching in the Song of Solomon? I know very few pastors who would dare to preach at all from the book. I can't say that I have been in a constant study of the Song of Solomon since then, but I can say that I have had an interest since then. Up to this point my only real exposure to this book of the Bible, other than reading it in my devotional time, had given me three insights: some critics of the past have claimed it should not be in the Bible because of its intimate nature, older students of the Bible use it as a picture of Christ's relationship to His church, and more recently teachers have begun to point to it for lessons concerning intimacy in the marriage relationship. I say recently, but I think I am talking about twenty-five or more years ago now. The first book I remember hearing about that used the Song of Solomon that way was, *What the Bible says about Love Marriage and Sex* by Dr. David Jeremiah. Jeremiah pastored what I thought was then a Fundamental Baptist Church in the San Diego area so, although I never bought the book, it caught my attention.

THE SETTING

Verse one gives me two important pieces concerning this book:

- **It tells me the author is Solomon**
- **It tells me the significance Solomon put on this book**

A. Solomon is said to be the wisest man that ever lived

God promised to give him wisdom. Solomon at times demonstrated wisdom and others testified of his wisdom. Solomon was the son of King David and the man who succeeded David on the throne of Jerusalem. He was wealthy. He was a peacetime leader and he was respected, but he was not a perfect man.

The Bible includes three books written by Solomon, they are all classified among the poetical books of the Bible as the books of wisdom. Those books, in the order we find them in the Bible are:

- **Proverbs**
- **Ecclesiastes**
- **Song of Solomon**

B. The Song of Solomon was Solomon's personal favorite

We call it the Song of Solomon. Solomon called it, "*The song of songs*". The Bible says that Solomon wrote three thousand proverbs and one thousand and five songs[2]. Not all of them are recorded in the Bible, of course, but of them all, this one was his favorite. It was, in his mind, the best that he has done. Better than the Proverbs. Better the Ecclesiastes.

C. One theory is that he wrote:

Song of Solomon in his youth before he had spoiled himself with many wives, Proverbs in the height of his life when wisdom and godliness ruled him, and Ecclesiastes near the end of his life, after the bitter experiences of sin and once he had come to his spiritual mind again. I prefer to leave the three books in the same order we find them in the Bible:
Proverbs is written over a period of time.
It is collection of his wisdom
Ecclesiastes is written in the zenith of his life.

By the end of Ecclesiastes, I believe we really can think of him as wise when he writes Ecclesiastes 12:13[3]

Song of Solomon, the final one, is the "Song of Songs." Written from the perspective of a man who has spoiled his love in sin and now writes a beautiful picture of true love WITH the key feature being its representation of the spiritual life

THE SUBJECT

The Song of Solomon is exactly what it says it is; a song. You and I might understand it better as a play. It is really a series of songs that each fit together to convey one story. It would be like an opera. In ancient history these sorts of "songs" were very common. Homer's Iliad and Odyssey would have each been performed like an opera. They were used as entertainment. They were used to make political statements. They often taught some sort of moral lesson and they were often used to portray some history. The Iliad and Odyssey, for instance, were set around the historical events of the Trojan Wars, but not an awful lot besides that should be considered historical facts. Odysseus never really met the Cyclops, the Sirens, or Poseidon. Just because some portions of his story is true doesn't mean we should believe that these mythical creatures actually existed.

View the Song of Solomon like a play, a musical. There are, in this play:
- **An actor**[4]
- **An actress and**
- **A choir**

THE SLANT

Among those who take the book seriously there are two approaches:
- **To view it as representing Christ's love for the church**[5]
- **To see it as teaching about healthy intimacy in marriage**

Almost all of the old timers in preaching called this book a representation of the love relationship of Christ or His church. Many of them did recognize the practical use of the book for

3

marriage too. J Vernon McGee[6] (perhaps the last of the "old timers") preached the picture as pre-eminent over the human relationship. McGee said that it does teach about human relationships; but it teaches *so much more*.

On the other hand, many of the more modern teachers not only prefer to focus on the human sexuality approach to understanding this book, they think it is nearly heretical to use it to address the subject of Christ and the church. In his message, **Preaching the Song of Songs:** How Should Pastors Handle, "Bellies," "Navels," and "Breasts," from Their Sunday Morning Pulpit?[7], Dr. Mark McGinniss, professor at Baptist Bible Seminary in Clark's Summit, Pennsylvania, very nearly accuses the use of the Song of Solomon to teach anything other than sexual intimacy as pastoral irresponsibility. The same can also be said of Skip Heitzig and Bill Creasy's works on the Song of Solomon.[8]

Dr. David Jeremiah does much the same when he writes,[9] "I understand that is what some say—that Song of Solomon is an Old Testament, metaphorical version of Ephesians 5:22-33, that it's not about human love and marriage but about divine love and the union of Christ and His "bride," the church. Various commentators have espoused this view of the book through the centuries. They've had a field day going over the imagery in all these verses and matching it up to New Testament principles. There's something to be said for that, and I've read some wonderful suggestions about the nature of Christ's love for His church based on Solomon's love for his bride. But I'm not prepared to embrace that view of the book myself—to de-sexualize the Song of Solomon. Our Scriptures work on many levels, but the presence of symbolism doesn't overrule literal meaning. In other words, we can read the book as a symbolic poem about Christ, but we should primarily read it at face value: as a song of love—romantic and emotional and sexual—between husband and wife."

I believe that much good can come from the study of the Song of Solomon for the married couple and would not hesitate to recommend a married couple read Dr. David Jeremiah's book. But I think he has succumbed to the spirit of our day, which places most of the emphasis on our needs and less on God's glory. I prefer the spirit of the old fashioned preacher who believed that when we place the emphasis on God's glory we will find that is really what we need.

August 14, 1836 a young preacher by the name of Robert Murray McCheyne preached a sermon as a candidate for the pastorate of a church. He chose Song of Solomon chapter 28-17 as his text. His opening words were, *"There is no book of the Bible which affords a better test of the depth of a man's Christianity than the Song of Solomon."*[10] That, my friends, will be the approach we take as we study our way through the Song of Solomon in the coming weeks.

[1] About 12 years ago at the time of this writing.
[2] 1 Kings 4:32
And he spake three thousand proverbs: and his songs were a thousand and five.
[3] Ecclesiastes 12:13
Let us hear the conclusion of the whole matter: Fear God, and keep his commandments: for this is the whole duty of man.
[4] I think there are actually two, the shepherd and Solomon. I do not believe that Solomon is the Shulamite girl's beloved.
[5] This was actually the Jewish interpretation too. They say the Song of Solomon as representing God's love relationship with His chosen people, Israel. They read from and used the Song of Solomon in their Passover celebrations.
[6] I would prefer to quote from and point you to more Baptist preachers than I have in this lesson but there just are not many who have preached much from this book and have published what they have done.
[7] https://outsidemydoor.files.wordpress.com/2013/01/mcginniss_preaching-the-song-of-songs-copy.pdf
[8] Both found as audible books on Audible.com
[9] In his introduction to *What the Bible says about Love Marriage and Sex*
[10] http://blog.christianfocus.com/index.php/2012/06/28/robert-murray-mccheyne-on-the-song-of-solomon/, accessed 9-18-14

Chapter 2

THE BOOK OF COMMUNION
Song of Solomon 1:1-4

Two similar but extreme positions may be taken with the Song of Solomon:
- **One might say that the book is too graphic to belong in the Word of God - it cannot be a holy book.**
- **Another might say that the book is too graphic to speak of spiritual things; that its value is strictly for the benefit of the earthly marriage.**

I want to suggest to you that neither of them is accurate and that they stem firstly from a perverted view of human love.
We are inundated with lusty things these days.

Not that immorality has not always existed, but that it has taken on new and ever increasing proportions:
1. At one time the only way a person could be enticed morally would be through an illicit relationship.
- **There was no printed word**
- **There was no photography**

There were lewd sculptures and paintings beginning just previous to the birth of Christ but they were not rare and certainly not available to everybody.

2. Then comes the printing press.
And for as much good as that technology has done, especially in getting the Word of God to men, Satan has used it as well. Even things as "seemingly innocent" as romance novels were preached much against in years gone by. Because, even if they are not graphic, they stir up passionate desires. Of course, many of those books are not even seemingly innocent.

3. Radio added voices to the storyline so now the mind need not imagine that sultry voice or, for the ladies, deep, masculine voice.

6

4. Then came the television and the movie house.

And, as art has always done, both pressed the envelope of decency from the very beginning - delivering as much sex as the public could consume without being overridden with guilt and giving up on the industry.

But the more they pressed the envelope, the more accustomed the public has become so that, today, the most modest of Christian thinks nothing of being entertained by sex.

5. Now we have the internet where the sex traffic is unrestrained.

Our children are exposed to sexual content from such an early age that 11 and 12 year olds are regularly caught "sexting" and posting provocative pictures of themselves online.

And what it has done is so messed up our concept of intimacy that we assume filth rather than virtue.

The problem with studying the Song of Solomon is that we are going to imagine things in this book that would not have been considered 150 years ago.

- **It's going to be difficult for some people to move past their fleshly thoughts to allow God to speak to their spirits.**
- **Some people are going to want to feed on those lustful imaginations rather than let God's Word instead feed their souls.**

But we have to do it.

We are losing the battle for the souls of spiritual men and women. Even in the very best of churches, preachers are often guilty of doing what is the safe thing, what is the expedient thing, what is the thing that will pacify and build a congregation, rather than striking at the heart of our sin trouble.

OUR PROBLEM IS THAT WE DO NOT LOVE CHRIST

Even in the best of churches, Christians have such a poor relationship with the Lord that they are embarrassed to love Him.

A preacher by the name of A.L. Newton published a book in 1858, called, *The Song of Solomon Compared with Other Scriptures.* In it he wrote, "Thus the book is full of Jesus. But it is Jesus in peculiar character.

- **He is not seen here as Saviour**
- **Nor as King**
- **Nor as High Priest**
- **Nor as Judge**
- **Nor as Prophet**
- **Nor as the Captain of our Salvation**
- **Nor as the great Shepherd of the sheep**
- **Nor as the mighty God**
- **Nor as the King of Kings**
- **Nor as His people's Surety**

- No! It is in a dearer and closer relation than any of these – it is Jesus as our Bridegroom, Jesus in marriage union with His bride, His Church."[1]

Our problem today is that the very best Christians we have know Jesus as all of the above, except as the lover of his or her soul. That must be corrected. We have got to address this great sin and return to passionate love with the Lord.

WHAT ABOUT THE SONG OF SOLOMON?

Quoting Newton again,

"The Song of Solomon is to be understood as the mutual interchange of affections of the Bridegroom and the Bride. It is the experience of the soul towards Christ in this particular relationship." Such an understanding of the Song of Solomon was pretty standard until even 25-30 years ago.

Pastor C.H. Spurgeon's favorite title for Jesus back in the 1850's was "My well beloved" (taken from Song of Solomon)

J.G. Bellett wrote sometime before 1909, "Let Him kiss me with the kisses of His mouth." She had been keeping the vineyards — attending to things abroad, but now was learning that her own vineyard had been neglected; and the deeper things of personal fellowship are longed for. The saint is leaving Martha's and taking Mary's place, longing to feed under His own eye and from His own hand, and not another's."

Pastor H.A. Ironside, wrote in about 1933 that the Song of Solomon is a"… singularly delightful portion of the Word of God."

The Song of Solomon is the story of the believer who longs to move from a mere servant of Christ to a lover of Christ.

Here is the question – **Can you handle intimacy with Jesus Christ?** Or will you settle to hold him, but at an arm's length? **Will you choose to maintain your awkward**, uneasy walk with the Lord? Or will you decide to take His arm, embrace His affections, and begin to pour out to Him your own? Will you settle to have Jesus as your *Saviour*, *King*, *Shepherd*, *High Priest* and *Captain*? Or will you take Him to be your Bridegroom, the lover of your soul?

HOW WILL WE DEAL WITH THE MUSHY DETAILS?

Mostly superficially. That is not to say I am going to deal with the Song of Solomon superficially. We will take every portion seriously. But I do not believe the book is meant to be taken literally. In Biblical hermeneutics the rule is to take everything in the Bible literally unless the text itself indicates it is to be understood otherwise. When Jesus, speaking about Herod, called him an old fox that does not mean that Herod walked on four legs and had a bushy tail. We understand he meant it metaphorically. I believe the same is true with the Song of Solomon. I am claiming, with the majority of preachers until twenty five years ago, that the Song of Solomon is a picture of Christ's love for His people.

It would be ridiculous to attempt to give a literal interpretation, for instance of verse two. We don't literally kiss Jesus on the mouth, nor does He kiss us on the mouth. The point is that people who are in love express that love without shame or embarrassment. The point is to verbally and emotionally express love for Jesus Christ and to expect that same love to be reciprocated.

[1] A.L. Newton, *The Song of Solomon Compared with Other Scriptures.* Introductory thoughts.

Chapter 3

THE MUSICAL
Song of Solomon 6:1-3

To my knowledge everyone who believes that the Song of Solomon is part of the Holy Scriptures, believe also that the Song of Solomon is really a series of songs; anywhere between two to thirteen of them.[1]

Think of it like one of the old musicals a lot of us grew up with:
- **Singing in the Rain**
- **White Christmas**
- **The Music Man**
- **Seven Brides for Seven Brothers or**
- **Oklahoma**

I want to try to acquaint you with the layout of the Song of Solomon by giving you three examples of how those divisions by song.

EXPLORING THE LOVE SONG OF SOLOMON
John Phillips

Philips is, I think, the most recent author I will use in my studies for these lessons. But he has passed away.[2] He agrees with me that Solomon is not the hero but the villain of the book. He divides the Song of Solomon into eight songs:

A. An hour of trouble
1:1-8
The Shulamite girl is abducted by Solomon.

B. An hour of temptation
1:9-11
Solomon attempts to entice her with his wealth.

C. An hour of tenderness
1:12-2:7

The Shulamite and the shepherd meet.

D. An hour of truth

2:8-3:5

The daughters of Jerusalem try to reason with her that marriage with Solomon would be better than with the shepherd.

E. An hour of talk

3:3-11

Solomon's friends speak with her about all the treasures of the King.

F. An hour of togetherness

4:1-5:1

The Shulamite and the shepherd are wed.

G. An hour of testimony

5:2-6:3

The couple have their struggles.

H. An hour of testing

6:4-8:4

The marriage has some enemies.

I. An hour of triumph

8:5-14

The Shulamite and her groom, together forever.

THE SEVEN CHURCHES OF ASIA

Someone[3] has pointed out parallel between the scenes in Song of Solomon and the seven churches of Asia in Revelation. There are three ways Bible students generally apply the lessons of those letters written to the seven churches:

1. Literally – there were literally seven churches in Asia and the Lord wrote to those churches.

That is obviously true. However, if we stop here all we have is historical content.

2. As representations – each church has a unique set of problems and a unique personality.

It is easy to see these same problems and personalities represented in churches today. Some churches have aspects from more than one of the seven.

3. As a calendar of Church history – each church represents a period of time from the founding of the church by Christ to the coming of Christ to begin the Tribulation period.

Ephesus is the first church; doctrinally pure but quickly losing its first love for Christ

Laodicea is the final period; when the church is lukewarm and Christ is really outside it.

I think there is value in applying the seven churches in all three approaches. We can see these same seven characteristics in the Song of Solomon.

A. Meeting
This parallels with the church at Ephesus.
They are in love but they have some problems.

B. Dating
Which parallels perhaps the church at Smyrna of which Jesus says they are impoverished but rich.

C. Courting
There is a section in the Song of Solomon where the couple are torn apart by the King, who has abducted her from her shepherd. This could be the church at Pergamos, who hold the doctrine of the Nicolaitans, which the Lord hates.

D. Wedding
The church at Thyatira. Jesus knew their works, charity, service, faith, patience and works again.
Marriage is work.

E. Living - he's gone, she misunderstands

There are only two churches Jesus says nothing good about. Sardis is the first of those. She has a name that she lives but she is dead.

There is one scene in the Song of Solomon that the couple is obviously in a spat. She has locked him out of the bedroom. He appeals to her to let him in. By the time she softens and opens the door he is gone.

F. Reviving

The church of Philadelphia is the only one of the seven churches Jesus has nothing against. Chapters about six and seven describe marriage about as good as it can get on this earth.

G. Retreating

The last church is Laodicea, of which Jesus says nothing good. But there is a good thing associated with it. It is just after the Laodicean church that Jesus calls the believers to heaven.

The Song of Solomon ends with a prediction of the coming Groom.

I plan to use:

A PLAY IN FIVE ACTS

The five acts (scenes of the play) will be[4]

A. Initial drawing to the Saviour

1:1-2:7

B. Conviction prior to salvation

2:8-3:5

C. The new Birth

3:6-5:1

D. The Church Age - while He is away

5:2-8:10

E. Heaven, Christ's return

8:13-14

---

[1] And it looks to me like practically *every* number in between them.

[2] I believe the date was July 25, 2010, making his passing more recent than J Vernon McGee

[3] I do not recall where I read or heard this. It was likely in one of the podcasts I listened to while driving from one meeting to the next and looking for material to help me with this study.

[4] This is preliminary I am sure and will be adjusted a bit at a time as we work our way through this book.

Section Two - Initial drawing to the Saviour

Chapter 4

LOVE AT FIRST SIGHT
Song of Solomon 1:2-7

It's interesting how attraction works, isn't it? A young lady will hear that a certain young man is interested in her and her reaction is "eeeewww" But she hears that a different young fellow is interested and her heart begins to pitter-patter. Admittedly, especially for the younger ones – some of that is due to social structure:

• **She may not like him because he isn't cute**

• **She might like this other one because he is a football star**

But sooner or later, real attachments have to do with attractions that are, very nearly unexplainable. It is a broken system, I think because of the corruption of sin, but it speaks to me of the fact that God has created a certain man for a certain woman.

And so it is with those who come to love Jesus Christ. It is unexplainable, almost mystical how:

• **One person can come to believe in and love the Lord Jesus Christ so much while**

• **Another one, will be totally disinterested in Christ and**

• **Still another one will be filled with repulsion and hatred for our Lord**

This mystery is so powerful that some have been led to believe that Jesus Christ calls some to salvation and others to the pits of eternal damnation.

I see it completely differently than that.

• **God's love for mankind is such that He desires all to be saved** but

• **Man's corruption is such that most refuse**

Our saga begins with the Shulamite girl. I notice three things about her right off the bat:

SHE IS OBVIOUSLY ATTRACTED
Vs 2-3

Since I am not a girl I obviously don't think like a girl, but I have heard that many girls begin dreaming of their wedding day years before they even meet a man to marry.

- **They have the colors of the wedding chosen**
- **They have the general theme of the wedding chosen**
- **They have their hope chest with their collection of things needed for their wedding**

This Shulamite is a romantic young lady.

A. She's dreaming about *kisses* and *ointments* and *love*.

I make no apologies for insisting that the Song of Solomon is exactly what it claims to be; a song. It is an allegory, a story. It has, I think, only a loose connection with anything that literally happened but it does teach, I am convinced, very real spiritual lessons.

B. The setting has this young lady dreaming of love – but it is as yet unrealized love.

I think we should see her as the one who is attracted to the Saviour, but not, as yet born again.

- **What is it that attracts a person to be saved?**
- **What is it that brings a person to love Jesus Christ?**

In my case, that attraction happened YEARS before I came to be a Christian. I did not fully understand that attraction, but after being saved I look back and am certain that God was wooing me to come to Him by the time I was nine or ten years old.

But notice in vs 3 that she is not the only one who is attracted.
"...therefore do the virgins love thee."

I do not believe God's wooing is exclusive to "the elect." But that *God so loved the world, that he* gave his only begotten Son, *that whosoever believeth in Him should not perish, but have everlasting life.*[1]

The Holy Spirit of God not only convicts "the elect" but Jesus said
John 16:8
...when he is come, he will reprove the world of sin, and of righteousness, and of judgment:

Again Jesus said, John 12:32
And I, if I be lifted up from the earth, will draw all men unto me.

C. That initial attraction to Christ is, I am convinced, universal.
It has to be trained out of us.

SHE ASKS TO BE DRAWN TO HIM
Vs 4

A. Here is the difference between those who are saved and those who are lost –
- **The attraction to Christ is universal**
- **The gospel of Christ is universal**
- **The desire of Christ for men to be saved is universal**

But the action of men upon God's wooing is individual.

Romans 3:11
There is none that understandeth, there is none that seeketh after God.

Deuteronomy 4:29
But if from thence thou shalt seek the LORD thy God, thou shalt find him, if thou seek him with all thy heart and with all thy soul.

Very few seek the Lord, but those that do seek Him with all their heart and soul, find Him. And when they find Him they find,
Acts 17:27
... he be not far from every one of us:

B. Notice that she isn't simply passively asking, but she is actively pursuing her love.

Vs 4

"...we will run after thee:..."

It isn't just *"I will run after thee"*. A relationship with the Lord is an individual/personal one, but it must never be acted out alone. God calls us to be part of a local church where we assemble together to exhort and provoke one another to love and to good works.

C. But she has a problem; the king has brought her into his chambers.

The king represents the prince of this world, Satan, and his own attractions. If God calls all of us to be saved and woos all men to Himself, why is it that so many do not get saved? It is because we are in this world and the love of the things of the world blind them to the attractions toward the Lord.

When Anita and I worked at the Bible College we lived in a world of young attractions.

- **Every girl on the campus hoped she would meet her future husband there**
- **Almost every boy hoped he would meet his wife**

It doesn't take very long before you can see those attractions beginning to be discovered and developed. But more often than we wished, we could also see people becoming attracted to someone who was obviously not the right fit. Nine times out of ten, you can't talk them out of a relationship once it has begun.

- **You can't tell them the one that they really should be trying to attract**
- **You would be considered an ogre if you tried to talk them out of the relationship they had already begun**

It was a pretty tough spot as a leader on the campus.

I think we see the same thing in the spiritual world. There are people who are obviously drawn to the things of the Lord but they are so "bedazzled" by the things of the world that they can't see it. Satan presents every pretty thing he has in front of the souls of men and women to blind them to God's love for them and to spoil them of their love for God.

To further "complicate" things

SHE FEELS SO UNWORTHY
Vs 5-6

She presents three reasons she feels unworthy:

A. She has been exposed
She has been outside – in the world. She has seen things she maybe should not have seen and has been seen of those who maybe should not have seen her.

The Bible says, Romans 12:1-2
I beseech you therefore, brethren, by the mercies of God, that ye present your bodies a living sacrifice, holy, acceptable unto God, which is your reasonable service.
And be not conformed to this world: but be ye transformed by the renewing of your mind, that ye may prove what is that good, and acceptable, and perfect, will of God.

But she has been conformed to this world.

B. She is black
Black is very often symbolical of sin. In the course of her life she has been exposed to the world and has taken on both the conformity and character of the world.

She has sinned.

C. She is unkempt
Vs 6
"...mine own vineyard have I not kept."

She hasn't prepared herself for a relationship with the Saviour as she should have. Things have come between her and the Lord.

After Adam and Eve sinned, they heard the voice of God and instinctively hid themselves. So she instinctively says, "***Look not upon me...***" She is no different than any other born of man.

Romans 3:12
They are all gone out of the way, they are together become unprofitable; there is none that doeth good, no, not one.

Conclusion

But this one *is* different.   .

Vs 7

She wants to know Him.

She reminds me of John 1:37-39

And the two disciples heard him speak, and they followed Jesus.
Then Jesus turned, and saw them following, and saith unto them, What seek ye? They said unto him, Rabbi, (which is to say, being interpreted, Master,) where dwellest thou?
He saith unto them, Come and see. They came and saw where he dwelt, and abode with him that day: for it was about the tenth hour.

There were hundreds, potentially thousands of people there when John the Baptist pointed to Christ as "*the Lamb of God which taketh away the sin of the world*" but these two wanted to know more.

They asked. Jesus answered.

[1] John 3:16

Chapter 5

DATES ON THE HILL
Song of Solomon 1:8-17

As we begin this lesson keep in mind two things: First, this passage is an allegory. This is not a literal event. It is meant to represent something other than what your imagination (and mine) want to make it out to be. It is a song or a play. It is meant to represent the love relationship of the Lord for His people.

Secondly, the first chapter represents a budding relationship and not one that is in full blossom. In verse seven the shulamite girl asked, ***"Tell me, O thou whom my soul loveth, where thou feedest, where thou makest thy flock to rest...."*** I have already pointed out the similarities between that question and the one asked by the disciples in John 1:37-38
And the two disciples heard him speak, and they followed Jesus.
Then Jesus turned, and saw them following, and saith unto them, What seek ye? They said unto him, Rabbi, (which is to say, being interpreted, Master,) where dwellest thou?

There were potentially thousands of people who heard John the Baptist say that Jesus was the Lamb of God that taketh away the sins of the world, but only these two followed Jesus. They were not believers yet. But they were drawn to the Lord.

Song of Solomon chapters 1:1 through 2:7 describe that budding relationship of the soul who is drawn to Christ but hasn't yet been saved.
- **I know that soul well as it was my own for many years.**
- **I knew God existed**
- **I knew Jesus Christ is God**
- **I wanted to have a relationship with Him**

But at the same time I was not saved and could easily be pulled back into sinful patterns.

THE SHUNAMITE'S QUESTION
Song of Solomon 1:7
Tell me, O thou whom my soul loveth, where thou feedest, where thou makest thy flock to rest at noon: for why should I be as one that turneth aside by the flocks of thy companions?

She wants to know something a little bit more than the common crowd seems to want to know.

A. Where thou feedest
Where do you feed your sheep? Sheep is a figure of the people of God – in New Testament terms, the Christians. What do the Christians feed on? That's the Bible – the Word of God.

B. Where thy flocks rest
In the New Testament this would be the local church. It's where we gather together for:
- **Shelter from the world**
- **Feeding on the Word**
- **Comfort from one another's company**

She's asking right now about all of the "mechanical" stuff about the faith.

And then she says,

C. I want to be there too
"*...Why should I be as one that turneth aside by the flocks of thy companions?*"

There are some other shepherds in the world. She is looking to join up with this shepherd's flock.

THE SHEPHERD'S REPLY
VS 8-14

A. You know these answers by knowing the Shepherd
Vs 8

Jesus said,
John 10:27
My sheep hear my voice, and I know them, and they follow me:

In effect the shepherd says, "If you don't know me yet, you don't belong in my flock. It's a biblical lesson taught throughout the New Testament. The church is to be made up only of saved and scripturally baptized members.

- **Others can observe**
- **Others can attend services**
- **Others can ask questions and find out what our faith is all about**

But the church membership belongs only to those who already know Jesus Christ as Saviour.

This is one of the reasons why Baptists have never accepted transferring members from Catholic, or Lutheran or Presbyterian or any other Protestant church for that matter.

- **They believe you join the church in order to belong to Jesus**
- **We believe only those who belong to Jesus can join the church**

B. The shepherd loves her even while she is outside his flock
Vs 9-13

Read John 3:16 with this,
For God so loved the world, that he gave his only begotten Son, that whosoever believeth in him should not perish, but have everlasting life.

The Song is describing in euphoric and rapturous terms the Shepherd – Christ's love for us – even before our salvation.

Romans 5:8
But God commendeth his love toward us, in that, while we were yet sinners, Christ died for us.

DATES ON THE HILLS
Vs 15-17

The conversation has returned to the Shulamite. At this point she is still not in the fold, but she is expressing her love for the shepherd anyway. If the passage seems a little "inappropriate" I think you might be sensing something here. She is outside – she has no real bond with the shepherd yet.

24

- **She speaks of a bed of green and beams and rafters of cedar and fir.**
- **She is talking about lying under a tree instead of inside a home.**

I think the picture is that she is dreaming of what could be and what we know will eventually be. But right now – she is not his.

I know a ton of people whose relationship with Christ is just about like that.
- **They talk about loving Him**
- **They speak about worshipping Him**

But they have never gotten saved and if they are saved, they have never joined His church.

Jesus said, John 14:15
If ye love me, keep my commandments.

That's going to mean
- **Scriptural baptism**
- **Church membership**
- **Faithful service to the Lord through that church**

Some people do get there. They are drawn to Christ, and though the process is not immediate for them, they do grow to embrace not only the "good feeling" of Christianity but the covenant relationship with Christ. But some never do. They just talk about how much they love Jesus without ever proving their love by becoming a true follower of Christ. Which are you?

Chapter 6

"LOVE SICK"
Song of Solomon 2:1-7

We last left our couple, the Shulamite girl and her shepherd love, on a date in the hills. They were not married yet, but she was dreaming.

Chapter 2 verses 1-7 give us a conversation in three persons:
- **First, the shepherd speaks to his Shulamite darling**
- **Second, the Shulamite speaks to her shepherd love**
- **Finally, the Shulamite speaks to "the daughters of Jerusalem"**

That this is a song or a play becomes obvious right here. The daughters of Jerusalem are not on the hills watching their date. This was a common theatrical tool used in Greek and Roman plays near the same era; the actors involve the audience, often times addressing them as if they are a part of the scene. This trick was often used in TV shows like Magnum PI, where he knowingly looks into the camera as if to include those watching the show in the action.

THE PERCEPTION OF THE SHEPHERD
Vs 1-2

Many commentaries (some people say the best commentaries) say that this verse is more than likely spoken by the female of the story. However not every commentary agrees and I think the flow of the passage as well as the sense of the text assigns these words to the same person who speaks verse 2, and that is certainly the male. Remember that this is an allegory. It represents:
- God's love for His people
- Christ's love for His church

She's daydreaming of what will be what is not yet a reality. They aren't married, and perhaps, not all of her thoughts are as pure as they ought to be.

Verses 1 and 2 draw a comparison between him and her.

A. He is the Rose of Sharon and the lily of the valleys

Two different flowers are referenced.
- **One is a singularly beautiful flower**
- **The other is glory of the valley meadows**

There are all sorts of different ways to view these flowers in reference to Jesus Christ.

I see Him first as,

1. The Rose, the most splendid of all flowers

I understand that the rose of Sharon was probably not like our rose today.

But I see the Bible as a living book. God knew we would read this passage in the United States of America and that we would picture a rose in a unique way.

It is more than acceptable to view this a representing Christ as the loveliest of all that are lovely.

2. The ornament of life – especially while in the valleys

Sometimes life gets the best of us and we all go through times in valleys.

Christ makes even those times bearable and beautiful

On the other hand, he says of her,

B. She is a lily among thorns

She is beautiful, but she is not a rose and she is among thorns (defined here as the daughters).

The believer, and especially the believer as he or she represents a part of a local church:
- **Is beautiful for salvation – having the righteousness of Christ**
- **Is still in the process of sanctification – not yet being perfected**

- **Is in the midst of the world of thorns – she must therefore take measures not to be choked by them.**

Matthew 13:3
And he spake many things unto them in parables, saying, Behold, a sower went forth to sow;

Matthew 13:7
And some fell among thorns; and the thorns sprung up, and choked them:

Matthew 13:22
He also that received seed among the thorns is he that heareth the word; and the care of this world, and the deceitfulness of riches, choke the word, and he becometh unfruitful.

In this case, however, she is still "*among the thorns*."
She isn't yet saved. That seed, as it were, has been sown, but it hasn't yet taken root and sprung to new life.

The scene now turns to the female where we see,

THE PASSION OF THE SHULAMITE
Vs 3-6

In verse five, she confesses her love sickness and gives us three pictures of Christ's care and support for her:
A. She sat under His shadow
Vs 3
Where she has delighted in the taste of His fruit.

B. She has come into His banqueting house
Vs 4
Where she experienced His love for her.

C. She has felt His embrace
Vs 6
And knows His love for her to be genuine and real.

I am going to suggest that:

- **The apple represents the Word of God by which we live**
- **The banqueting house represents the local church where believers find shelter from the world**
- **The embrace represents the fellowship of the saints which serves to comfort, support and strengthen us in our faith**

But she still isn't saved.

Hebrews 6:4-6

For it is impossible for those who were once enlightened, and have tasted of the heavenly gift, and were made partakers of the Holy Ghost,
And have tasted the good word of God, and the powers of the world to come,
If they shall fall away, to renew them again unto repentance; seeing they crucify to themselves the Son of God afresh, and put him to an open shame.

There is such a thing as a person who has experienced all of this:

- **The love of God**
- **The blessing of His Word**
- **The fellowship of the saints**

But is not a true Christian.

We spoke a minute ago about the lily among the thorns and the seed that is sown among the thorns but the life is quickly choked out.

People very often ask whether the seed sown among the thorns is saved and just dies out or is not really saved at all.

That is exactly my point – you never know.

I just did a personal study in my walk with God a couple of weeks ago where I found that Jesus taught that a little bit of Christianity is not enough.

The Christian faith is an all or nothing proposition.

Are you certain you are all in?

The final section still has the female voice but her audience is changed

THE PRONOUNCEMENT TOWARDS THE OUTSIDERS
Vs 7

In a romantic relationship between a man and woman there is a point where certain expressions of love are not yet appropriate. Some people in our world today would disagree with that.
- **We have a huge number – perhaps the majority, who sleep together before their wedding**
- **We have a number of them who will live together outside of marriage**
- **We have plenty of others who will encourage them in doing so**

There is a secondary lesson found here which is that those passions should not be encouraged before the right time. Measures ought to be taken to ensure that a man and woman who are not married don't stir up passions that should only be expressed in marriage.

We have something similar in the spiritual world where so called Christians of all sorts of denominations encourage a relationship with Christ that is not yet appropriate.
- **Baptism prior to salvation is not appropriate**
- **Church membership before Scriptural baptism is not appropriate**
- **Partaking in the Lord's Supper before membership in a sound local church is not appropriate**

The fleshly side of man says
- **"I want these things!**
- **I want them now!**
- **I don't want to have to wait!"**

And the religious "**daughters of Jerusalem**" chime in with them and say, "You shouldn't have to wait. If you want them, take them. If one church won't give them to you, come to us – we will."

I want every man woman and child to receive every blessing the Lord could possibly give them:

- **I want them saved – but that won't come without repentance**
- **I want them baptized – but that won't come without salvation**
- **I want them to be members of Christ's local church – but that won't come without Scriptural baptism**
- **I want them to experience the blessing of the Lord's Supper – but that won't come without church membership**

Section Three - Conviction prior to salvation

Chapter 7

DRAWN IN
Song of Solomon 2:8-17

John 10:27
My sheep hear my voice, and I know them, and they follow me:

With Song of Solomon 2:8 we enter into the second act or scene in our "Musical." I call this scene "**Conviction prior to salvation**" or the "**Calling prior to salvation**."
John 6:44 says,
No man can come to me, except the Father which hath sent me draw him: and I will raise him up at the last day.

Every man, woman and child is called of God to salvation. The youngest of children have a sense of this calling of God and desire to know Him. It is only after conditioning and conformity to this world that the innate love for God becomes covered over with the scar of worldly living. God's call continues and, in some circumstances, breaks through the build up of worldly scarring – and one here and another there, begins to hear the voice of their beloved.

This scene will have two parts:
She's heard His Voice
2:8-17
She seeks Him until she finds Him
3:1-5

Just after I became a Christian my pastor told me about an evangelistic program that was going around a few years earlier. It was called "I Found It." The idea was that people would have bumper stickers, and lapel pins and t-shirts that had the phrase, "I found it" on them. Passersby would become curious. Then Christians were encouraged to go out door knocking or go through the phone book calling people and simply say, "I found it!" Assuming the person you contacted had seen the phrase somewhere, they would respond, "Found what?" To which you would say, "I found eternal life through Jesus Christ." Pastor told me that there had been a pretty big stink about it because, according to the program's detractors, the Bible doesn't say that we find Christ but that He finds us.

In reality, the Bible makes it clear that the seeking and finding happen from both sides. Jesus said Luke 19:10
For the Son of man is come to seek and to save that which was lost.

On the other hand Paul preached, Acts 17:27
That they should seek the Lord, if haply they might feel after him, and find him, though he be not far from every one of us:

The first half of this act is His seeking her. The second half is her seeking Him.

SHE HEARS HIS VOICE
Vs 8-9
Jesus said, "*My sheep hear my voice...*" What a wonderful thing when a soul hears the voice of God calling to them. It is nothing a man can do:
- **We can witness**
- **We can pray, but**
- **We cannot make them hear the voice of the Lord.**

A. A drastic realization
"Behold, He cometh"

When a person comes to the point of salvation, one of the very first things they realize is that – Jesus IS coming. They are going to meet Him. Either:
- **They will be saved or**
- **They will be lost**

But they will not avoid meeting Christ. He will come to receive them or He will come to judge them, but He is coming either way.

At this realization, we then find listed these
B. The qualities of His person

1. What He is doing
Vs 8
Leaping and skipping upon the mountains and hills. Several things are represented here:
- **His power**
- **His swiftness**
- **His sense of victory**

2. Who He is like
Vs 9
A roe or young hart; Both of them are in the deer/sheep family. My Saviour came first of all as a lamb to take away the sins of the world.

3. Where He is
Vs 9

I am reminded of Revelation 3:20
Behold, I stand at the door, and knock: if any man hear my voice, and open the door, I will come in to him, and will sup with him, and he with me.

The point being that He is waiting for us to invite Him in to our lives.
- **He will not force Himself**
- **He will not make us be saved**
But He is there as soon as we invite Him.

HE SPAKE AND SAID
Vs 10-15
Look at this portion as the soul winner's work… This is her report of what He said to here; "She said, he said." I find four instructions to her from Him:

A. Rise Up
Vs 10, 13

A Christian is called to be separate and distinct from this world. He or she is also called to be:

- **Holy**
- **Undefiled**
- **To walk worthy of the vocation of our faith.**

As a witness for Jesus Christ, our task is not to beg people to make some sort of profession, any sort of profession of faith in Christ; my mission is to point them to the Saviour who will lift them from the dunghill to a throne.

B. Come Away
Vs 10, 13

2 Corinthians 6:17
Wherefore come out from among them, and be ye separate, saith the Lord, and touch not the unclean thing; and I will receive you,

God always calls Christians to come away, to come out from among the people of the world – to come away:

- **From winter to spring**
- **From darkness to light**
- **From cold to warm**
- **From death to life**
- **From fruitlessness to fruitfulness**

C. Be seen and heard
Vs 14

When the three Hebrews stood out from the crowd, refusing to bow before Nebuchadnezzar's idol, When they spoke up and said, "Our God is able to deliver us from the fiery furnace, but even if He doesn't we will not bow."

- **Who do you suppose thought they looked beautiful?**
- **Who do you suppose enjoyed hearing them the most?**

When you rise up, come away from the world, and stand out for Jesus Christ, it is the Lord Himself who sees that as beautiful.

D. Careful for spoilers
Vs 15

This verse sounds a lot like Matthew 13:19
When any one heareth the word of the kingdom, and understandeth it not, then cometh the wicked one, and catcheth away that which was sown in his heart. This is he which received seed by the way side.

It's up to you and me to take away the "little foxes" that will spoil what God is doing in us.

SHE BEGS FOR HIS LEADING
Vs 16-17

A. She declares her allegiance
Vs 16
There comes a certain place in every person's life when they have to go all in for Jesus Christ or not.

Billy Sunday was a professional baseball player and a self professed drunk. One afternoon he and a bunch of his drunken buddies happened by a street corner where a group from the Pacific Garden Rescue Mission in Chicago were out witnessing. Sunday's buddies began to mock and jeer the group. According to Sunday's own testimony he spoke up to his friends and said, "This is where we part company boys." And he joined up with the people at the mission.

B. She acknowledges His absence
Vs 16-17
Though there is a drawing to the Lord, she isn't connected to him yet. He is feeding in the lilies, waiting for the break of day.

C. She seeks His soon coming
Vs 17
Whether this is the return or Christ of not is difficult to say. There is a lot of "discussion" over just what are the mountains

of Bether. I am going to take this, at this point, as that point in a person's life when:

- **They are under conviction**
- **The seed of God's Word has been planted in their heart**
- **They have tasted the good fruit of the Word of God**

But they haven't been born again.

I don't believe it is ever as sudden as it seems to be in some people. Though being born again is a sudden and momentary thing, I think I have observed that in the case of everywhere a person calls upon the Lord and makes an obvious change in life, you find out that God's Holy Spirit had been working on them for quite some time.

When Apostle Paul met Jesus on the road to Damascus, Jesus said to him, *"it is hard for thee to kick against the pricks."* God's Spirit had been dealing with him for some time. But when he met Jesus Christ – that moment of salvation was a sudden one.

Chapter 8

SHE SEEKS HIM
Song of Solomon 3:1-5

While I have always had an interest in spiritual things, what I remember most about my earlier years was that God sought me. God brought witness after witness into my life:

- **A backyard Bible school when I was in third or fourth grade**
- **A friend who got saved when I was in seventh grade**
- **An invitation to a youth group when I was a teenager**
- **A showing of a Billy Graham crusade when I was in high school and**
- **A witness from a co-worker not long after I had graduated from high school**

But I can tell you that, though it did not happen quickly, there came a day when I began to seek God.

It happened some time shortly after high school. Cash Nichols and another fellow there, whose name I do not remember, began to witness to me. After I teased them for witnessing, I returned to them to ask how to be saved. When they were not able to give me a clear answer, I began searching for myself. I wanted to be a Christian. It is this that I believe we see in Song of Solomon 3:1-5.

- **The Shepherd has sought her in chapter 2:8-17**
- **She responds by seeking him in these verses**

THE SEEKING HEART
Vs 1-2

Jeremiah 29:13
And ye shall seek me, and find me, when ye shall search for me with all your heart.

A. **I am evaluating my own struggle to salvation** as we go through this book and in my case I think there were several phases:

1. **An initial interest as a child – I believe every child has this**

2. A stage of skepticism and rejection – this stage is brought about, I believe, by the various forms of conformity to the world

3. A stage of interest, but not from the heart – America is full of people who profess belief in Christ, but it is not a hearty faith

4. A stage of blindness and rejection – this is the work of the enemy of our soul, Satan.

5. A stage of earnest, heartfelt desire to know Jesus Christ as Saviour

I think the difference between those whose lives are changed by their faith and those who claim to have a faith but bear no spiritual fruit is a difference of the heart:

- **Many people have an intellectual profession of Christ**
- **Much fewer have a heart possession of Christ**

Here is the lesson I believe we learn in this text –

B. The soul that seeks Jesus will not be disappointed

Acts 10:1-3

There was a certain man in Caesarea called Cornelius, a centurion of the band called the Italian band,
A devout man, and one that feared God with all his house, which gave much alms to the people, and prayed to God alway.
He saw in a vision evidently about the ninth hour of the day an angel of God coming in to him, and saying unto him, Cornelius.

Cornelius has the right heart. He seeks for God and he is not disappointed. God sent Peter to tell him how to be saved.

- **It's not good enough to be sincere**
- **It's not good enough to want to know the Lord**

A person has to be born again. God saw to it that someone was there to tell him how to be saved.

I believe this is the case of every man, woman or child

- **In any land**
- **During any century**
- **At any time**
- **Under any circumstances**

God, I am sure, has seen to it that there was someone to witness to them.
- That's true of people in China
- That's true of the Indians in America
- That's true of the aborigine in Africa or Australia

How He did it, I do not know Who He sent, in most cases I do not know But that He did it, I have no doubt.

WATCHMAN
Vs 2-3

A. It's dangerous for a girl to go out about the city at night – even if she has good reason.

It's also a dangerous time when a person begins to seek Christ in earnest because Satan is more than willing to give them something false.

I got saved watching a TV program. Very shortly afterward, the Jehovah's Witnesses came to my house. They asked me if I had any interest in spiritual things. I told them that as a matter of fact, I had just become a Christian. They asked me if I was interested in having an in home Bible study, something to this day I am opposed to, but then I said yes, not knowing who they were. They came to my home for several weeks before I got uneasy about them and quit letting them in.

After that a man moved in next to me and befriended me. He was a "self proclaimed" evangelist. He did not believe in any one church or denomination.
- He travelled around the country, living in his little trailer with his huge family.
- He would pull up to a park, climb on top of his suburban and begin playing his guitar until he had a group, at which time he would begin to preach.
- He visited all of the churches in the area, mostly trying to get money from them.

Finally I just got discouraged, and although I never forgot that I got saved, just quit trying to do the right thing.

There is a reason Christ built the church and gave us preachers in those churches -

B. Ethiopian Eunuch

Acts 8:29-31

Then the Spirit said unto Philip, Go near, and join thyself to this chariot.
And Philip ran thither to him, and heard him read the prophet Esaias, and said, Understandest thou what thou readest?
And he said, How can I, except some man should guide me? And he desired Philip that he would come up and sit with him.

The Eunuch
- **Has the desire**
- **Has the location (Jerusalem), he even,**
- **Has the Bible**

But he still doesn't have the truth of Jesus Christ. He needs some man to guide him.

We have a terrible problem in Christianity right now where so many people think they can be students without guides.
- **Christians starting conversations meant to stir controversy**
- **Others spouting opinions without reservations**
- **No one qualified or asked to guide and direct the conversation toward the truth**

She couldn't find her shepherd without the watchman.

Once she spoke with the guide, the watchman, verse 4 says it was "*but a little*" until she "*found him whom my soul loveth:*"

When she found him the Bible says,

SHE WOULDN'T LET GO

Vs 4-5

The Christian faith is not meant to be a casual, take it or leave thing. It is meant to be "all or nothing"
- **It was all or nothing for God who so loved the world He gave is only begotten Son**
- **It was all or nothing for Jesus who gave His life to take away our sins**
- **It was all or nothing for Stephen, who was stoned to death praying for his murderers' forgiveness**
- **It was all or nothing for James who was beheaded in prison**
- **It was all or nothing for each of the Apostles, who gave their lives for Christ**

41

- It was all or nothing for the believers who were torn apart by wild beasts, and lit on fire to light the streets of Rome and tortured to death rather than deny the name of Christ
- It was all or nothing for John Wycliffe who labored alone and in secret to translate the Bible into the language of the common Englishman and was then killed for the work that he did
- It was all or nothing for those who were burned at the stake in Smithfield, England whose only crime was that they believed the Bible rather than the religion of the Queen
- It was all or nothing John Bunyon who spent eleven years in prison instead of accepting the King's license to preach the Bible Baptist Church

These people, and a million more thought their faith in Christ was something far to precious too let go even at pain of death.

Song of Solomon 3:4 could be viewed as the moment of salvation. Verse five reminds us once again that faith is in the pleasure of Christ.

Christianity
- Isn't a doctrine commanded by the laws of men
- Isn't a religion forced upon a man by one church or the other

Christianity is a relationship of love between the heart and soul of the believer and the Beloved Saviour of our soul.

Section Four - The New Birth

Chapter 9

WARNING: YOU'VE BEEN BORN AGAIN

Song of Solomon 3:6-11

Who is this that cometh out of the wilderness like pillars of smoke, perfumed with myrrh and frankincense, with all powders of the merchant?

Behold his bed, which is Solomon's; threescore valiant men are about it, of the valiant of Israel.

They all hold swords, being expert in war: every man hath his sword upon his thigh because of fear in the night.

King Solomon made himself a chariot of the wood of Lebanon.

He made the pillars thereof of silver, the bottom thereof of gold, the covering of it of purple, the midst thereof being paved with love, for the daughters of Jerusalem.

Go forth, O ye daughters of Zion, and behold king Solomon with the crown wherewith his mother crowned him in the day of his espousals, and in the day of the gladness of his heart.

The way that I see it, the picture of salvation, the new birth, happens in Song of Solomon 3:4. The Shulamite
- **Found her shepherd**
- **Held on and would not let him go**
- **Brought Him to her mothers chamber**

So begins the third of our five scenes or acts in the play that is the Song of Solomon.

The section of this "Song of Songs" that I am going to call the new birth covers chapters 3:6-5:1. But don't get the idea that, just because the Shulamite and the shepherd are married, that the heroine of the epic, is now saved, that everything is going to be wonderful from here on out. The Christian life is liken to a marriage. It's one of the reasons why we Christians need to fight so fervently for the sanctity of marriage these days.
- **Same sex marriage**
- **Premarital sexual relationships**
- **Living together outside of marriage**

- **Easy divorce**

all pervert the picture marriage is supposed to represent – the picture of Christ's love for His church.

You will remember that I have claimed that Solomon is not the shepherd of this story – the object of the Shulamite's love, but an antagonist, a rival to her true love. Accepting that Solomon is an enemy - a picture of the world in this case, what we find in Song of Solomon 3:6-11 is an instance of their very first threat to the Shulamite's relationship to her true love.[1]

The metaphor this is the first danger of the born again.

Not long after Anita and I moved to Denver to attend Bible College, I went out on visitation with the people of South Sheridan Baptist Church. We hadn't been in town even a whole week and we had not joined the church, but I wanted to be out witnessing so I showed up Thursday night and was assigned a visitation partner whom I had never met. We were given a visit to make so we headed to the car. I did not know Denver yet so he drove. It was probably 20 minutes or more from the church to the home that we were going to and in that half hour my partner had not said a word. Not one word. I even wondered if he could talk. I was a young Christian, but I was called to preach and figured that his lack of speaking meant that I was going to have to take the lead on this visit. We got to the house.

- **I knocked on the door**
- **Introduced the two of us to the couple**
- **Asked if we could come in for a few minutes**

The couple showed us into their living room where I gave them the plan of salvation and asked them if they would like to call upon the Lord to be saved. They said yes and we bowed our heads for them to pray and ask Christ to save them. Just then the living room door opened and a relative of theirs came bounding in unannounced and uninvited.

As I recall, he may have sat down and gotten saved too. It was not until we walked out of the house that my visitation partner spoke for the first time that night. He said, "**Satan always tries to destroy a newly saved person as soon as he can.**"

I have never forgotten that.

And I have seen it happen time and time again that, if Satan can't keep him out of Heaven, he will keep him out of Canaan (victorious Christian living). I don't know how many young Christians I have seen spiritually destroyed by:

A FALSE FAITH
Vs 6-7

There are two things in these verses that point to religion:
A. The utensils
Vs 6
- **Pillars of smoke**
- **Perfume**
- **Myrrh**
- **Frankincense**

These are all religious items and symbols of religion and worship.

B. The bed
Vs 7

God speaks of idolatry as a form of adultery. The Bible says in, Ezekiel 23:37
That they have committed adultery, and blood is in their hands, and with their idols have they committed adultery, and have also caused their sons, whom they bare unto me, to pass for them through the fire, to devour them.

Those false faiths, especially ones like:
- **Mormons**
- **Jehovah's Witnesses**
- **Church of Christ**

Who have a historical connection to Baptists and love to claim their conquests, especially over Baptists.

A FEAR OF FAITH
Vs 8
Notice the swords.

There are dangers associated with Christianity
- **Loss of friends and relationships**
- **Loss of respect in the workplace**
- **Loss of income, if your employment is unbecoming to Christ**

I had not been pastoring very long. We were still meeting in our old abandoned gas station, Probably had about 15 people attending our services, when a young family Haynes, I believe was their name, visited our Sunday morning services. I had never met them before - but when I gave the invitation she came forward to be saved. I led her to the Lord at the altar and, as I was taught to do, encouraged her to be baptized immediately. She agreed. I baptized her that morning and went to visit with the family the following week.

When I go to the house her most pressing concern was that she was a bartender and had quit her job because she knew a Christian shouldn't work there. I didn't tell her. She knew it already. I promise you, I never made it an issue. I never spoke about it or preached about it. But after two or three months of looking for a different job, and being unsuccessful, she went back to work at the bar and would never come to church again. Satan attacked her in her most vulnerable place – how she made a living.

AN AFFLUENT FAITH
Vs 9-10

I read these verses and hear
- **Wealth**
- **Affluence**
- **Money**

When I was a teen leader, we had a young man in our group who was absolutely obsessed with making money. His dad was about the same, but his dad had pretty much failed at it. This young man wanted to succeed. I am not sure he ever spoke to either Anita or me that he did not ask us if God was opposed to Christians being wealthy. He just could not stand it. He wanted to be rich – at any cost .

Not too long ago a young preacher my family is fairly close to quit the ministry and moved across the country, just to get away from the pressure of being a preacher. He had a good church, but he struggled financially. His dad, also a pastor, had also struggled financially. He saw other pastors succeeding and concluded that God just did not like his family.

More often though in preacher homes, I see something a little different. I see them compromise conviction for the sake of success. It's called pragmatism – church growth at any price.
- **Whatever music brings in the group**
- **Whatever Bible pleases the most people**
- **Whatever doctrines are less likely to offend**

They will justify themselves by pointing out how many attend their church and how many professions of faith they have had and how much influence they have in their community. But the truth is, they threw out their love of the Shepherd for their love of Solomon. They chose the wealth of this instead of the truth of God's Word.

And all they have built is just wood, hay and stubble.

A FLAMBOYANT FAITH
Vs 11

I see the daughters of Jerusalem behaving like a line of Las Vegas chorus girls, singing the praises of Solomon and his splendor. I am not saying that Solomon is always a negative picture in the Bible. Jesus spoke of him in positive terms. But even in those positive terms, there is a hint of the flamboyant. Matthew 6:29
And yet I say unto you, That even Solomon in all his glory was not arrayed like one of these.

Notice the words glory and arrayed. It's speaking about his clothing.
I have a friend whose church benefitted from the fallout of the flamboyance of some of the preachers of the eighties.
- **Jim and Tammy Faye Bakker**
- **Jimmy Swaggart**

The opulence and lifestyles of these guys became so infamous in the late 1980's that several very large churches associated with them felt a huge fallout. One of these super large charismatic churches in a large city where my friend is a pastor had two congregations meeting in two very nice church facilities. But their attendances in both churches had so declined that they elected to combine their congregations once again and sell one of the buildings. They were desperate to sell, so when my friend toured the facility, he told them that he could only pay a fraction of what they were asking. At first they refused but then came back and agreed, but stipulated they would take all of the furnishings to sell and recoup some of the difference. My friend said it had to be exactly as is or he would not buy. They refused, but then they contacted him again and had changed their minds.

What had happened was people were leaving their churches because these flamboyant ministries had turned them off to the faith. The
- **Benny Hinns**
- **Joel Osteens**

Are always going to be out there. And Satan will use them to suck people away from the faith if he can do it.

Conclusion

One of the first things a new Christian needs to know is that he now has an enemy. And at least at first, he is probably not going to show up in an Armored Personnel Vehicle. Most likely he is going to appear as an angel of light, luring the unsuspecting child of God away from a solid congregation where he can devour them spiritually in some sort of shallow, meaningless church wanna-be.

---

[1] I realize that many people see this as a splendid portrait of the beauty of Jesus Christ. This passage is the strongest argument that Solomon is in fact the object of the Shulamite's love and a type of Christ in this Song. I remain convinced that, given his philandering reputation, Solomon is an unlikely type of Christ in this instance.

Chapter 10

TRUE LOVE
Song of Solomon 4:1-15

If we were at a major play or an opera we would call our location "Scene 4, Act 10". The title for the scene is, "The New Birth". The Shulamite marries her shepherd love in chapter 3:4. Immediately some trouble happens. (chapter 3:6-11)

- **For her, she has Solomon trying to lure her away**
- **For you and me, Satan will attempt anything to keep Christians from growing in their relationship with the Lord**

I know that not everyone's experience is exactly like mine, but perhaps to no surprise to any of you, what I find in the Song of Solomon is remarkably like what has been my experience:

- **Before I became a Christian**
- **During that period when I became interested in Christianity**
- **After I did become a born again believer**

I did face temptations immediately after getting saved that almost ruined me. Praise the Lord for His grace that pulled me back into a walk with Christ!

- **I got saved watching a television evangelist in April of 1977.**
- **I began attending a start up Independent Baptist Church and was baptized there in December of 1979.**

My "chapter 3:6-11" phase lasted 2 ½ years. I believe it would have been a much shorter period of testing had I gotten saved through the ministry of a local Baptist church rather than a TV ministry. I praise the Lord that I heard the gospel and got saved. But I am convinced that I might not have had to struggle as I did in my first years as a Christian if I was connected with a local church. But when I did get connected, I am telling you – the first few years especially, were fantastic.

That's Song of Solomon 4:1-15. I am calling it "True Love".

WHAT ABOUT THE SENSUAL?

I don't believe we need to be embarrassed about anything that is written in the Word of God. The passage is sensual, but it's only graphic if you make it that in your head. If someone walked up to you and said, "Let me introduce you to my lover." What would you think? Almost certainly you would think of an immoral sexual relationship. But as recently as the 1950's they would be speaking about their boyfriend or girlfriend. The nature of our culture creates a graphic image out of something that is not necessarily graphic at all.

To be sure, passages like Song of Solomon 4:5
Thy two breasts are like two young roes that are twins, which feed among the lilies.
seems suggestive. But then again, Song of Solomon 4:2
Thy teeth are like a flock of sheep that are even shorn, which came up from the washing; whereof every one bear twins, and none is barren among them.
would spoil any romantic mood.

The modern Bible teacher, who wants to use the Song of Solomon as an excuse to make his ministry R rated, will try to convince you that girls four thousand years ago liked it when their husband called
- **Their teeth sheep (verse 2)**
- **The chest mountains (verse 6)**

I think it is more likely that a girl wouldn't like being described in those terms any more then than they would today.

WHAT DOES IT ALL MEAN?

Remember that this whole book is a series of songs. It is a musical play. Rather than viewing it is a literal/historical event it is to be viewed as a metaphor of the Christian relationship with Christ.

If you have ever read Pilgrim's Progress, I think you would be on the right track if you understood the Song of Solomon in the same way we would understand the Pilgrim's Progress.

What that means is that I don't think we have to find a meaning for every detail of this passage. Some teachers, for instance, say that verse one is Solomon (they see him as the hero of the story) describing these black goats that they say still live on the side of Mount Gilead. They make a big deal out of describing those goats running down the side of the mountain in the evening time, the setting sun illuminating them as they hop over rocks and crevices on their way down to the lower meadows. They say this is Solomon describing his lover's curly black hair glistening in the evening sunlight, dancing on her head as she so gracefully moves about. That being the case, verse two must be praising her because she brushes her teeth and none of them are missing!

I don't believe you have to do any of that with this text. It's just describing how much our Saviour loves us and how pleasant it is to be with Him.

I have to tell you, especially early on in my Christianity[1] were some wonderful days for me. The first Independent Baptist church I ever attended was Cornerstone Baptist Church in Kennewick, WA. Mike Riggs invited me. I was there the second Sunday of the church's existence. It would not have been chance that, just previous to that, I met Anita and was fast falling in love with her.

There were three of us in this very small church of only about 10-12 people who were young men about the same age. One was already divorced and attended church by himself. My friend's wife was, at that time, unsaved, and did not come to church, and I was single – Anita lived about 35 miles away. It was Mike and Mike and Marvin
- **We sat at church together**
- **We sang the hymns together**
- **We did things outside of church together**

It was an incredible time.

And while all of that was happening, Anita and I were getting serious and were married before I had been attending Cornerstone a year.

- **I became the church treasurer**
- **I taught a junior boys SS class**
- **Anita started attending the church with me and was soon baptized there**

After we got married we changed churches. In order that Anita would not have to drive the 35 miles to work I rented a place in Hermiston and drove the 60 miles or so to Hanford. We joined Bible Baptist Church of Hermiston.

- **I became the teen leader**
- **I shortly surrendered to preach and after about a year in Hermiston,**
- **We were headed to Bible College**

I can't say that everything that happened went perfectly. We were sorely tried during that year in Hermiston too. But I can testify that it truly felt like verse nine was Christ's words to Anita and me:

Song of Solomon 4:9

Thou hast ravished my heart, my sister, my spouse; thou hast ravished my heart with one of thine eyes, with one chain of thy neck.

There was a song on the Christian radio back then that went,
            If He keeps on blessing and blessing
                If he keeps on pouring it on
            If His love just keeps on getting richer
                If He keeps on giving a song
            If my cup gets fuller and fuller
            If my prayers keep on getting through
                If it keeps getting better and better
            Oh Lord, I don't know what I'm gonna do[2]

We would hear that song on the radio, sing along and literally say to each other – THAT'S EXACTLY HOW WE FEEL! God poured out His love upon us.

- **Time and again**
- **Over and over**

- **In ways that were unimaginable**

That's not to say we didn't have trouble too
- **We lost two babies**
- **I lost my job**
- **Anita had to have a tumor removed**
- **We almost died in a propane poisoning accident**

Satan tried for all his worth to keep us from victorious Christian living. But the Lord just kept pouring out His love and His grace. And we knew it. That's all you need to do with this passage.

WHERE WILL IT ALL END?

Song of Solomon 4:7
Thou art all fair, my love; there is no spot in thee.

I wonder if anyone can think of a passage that reminds you of?
Ephesians 5:25-27
Husbands, love your wives, even as Christ also loved the church, and gave himself for it;
That he might sanctify and cleanse it with the washing of water by the word,
That he might present it to himself a glorious church, not having spot, or wrinkle, or any such thing; but that it should be holy and without blemish.

Well, the Christian life has gone on now. Anita and I have 35 years since we entered into this Christian life. We have had lots of struggles and trials. We have also had lots of –we think – miraculous blessings where the Lord has poured out more favor on us than we could have ever dreamed.
- **There have been mountain top experiences and**
- **There have been depths of the valleys**

But in it all I have confidence that God's purpose is to make us *without spot or wrinkle or any such thing.*

This whole thing will end, Christian, with you in the presence of the Lord not having spot, or wrinkle, or any such thing but you will be holy and without blemish.

[1] Remember, this passage depicts the Shulamite and the Shepherd very shortly after their wedding.
[2] Bill Gaither

Chapter 11

LIVING BY FAITH
Song of Solomon 4:16-5:1

In the last chapter we addressed those immediate blessings after the New Birth. There were some challenges as Satan tries to keep a Christian from growing[1], but having gone through them, the blessings became obvious and abundant. Like the demoniac of Gadara, we are *"sitting and clothed and in our right mind."*[2] I imagine we thought, when we first became Christians, it would always be this way. The garden of God's fellowship is sweet and satisfying and constant.

- **The Bible is there every day**
- **Prayer is there every day**
- **Church services are a blessing and there several times a week**

Just like clockwork we can count on those things of God:

- **The preaching of the gospel**
- **The urging to growth**
- **The exhortations to separation from sin**
- **The provoking to witness**
- **The prayer meetings**
- **The revival meetings**
- **The missions emphasis**
- **It never changes**
- **The music is old fashioned**
- **The songs are a hundred years old**
- **The same people teach the same Sunday school classes**

I think the scene depicted in Song of Solomon 4:15-5:1 is that of the faithful Christian life; walking by faith and not by sight.

Two elements to this scene:
A PRAYER
Song of Solomon 4:16

A. The prayers are for both north winds and south winds to blow and stir up the fragrances of the spices of her garden.

She's asking for the winds to come from both directions

- **from above**
- **from below**

I think it relates to a metaphor used more often in our day using

- **mountains**
- **valleys**

- **High times**
- **Low times**

The truth is that Christian life is comprised of both, isn't it? I haven't ever met a person who has all high times. Neither have I met a person who has only low times.

It is observable that some people have more high times than low times and others have more low times than high but all of us have a blend of the two. The key is to benefit through them both:

- **To grow in grace when the south winds blow; to grow in humility when the winds come from the north.**
- **To glorify God when things when the north winds bring in blessings upon blessings. To praise the Lord and give Him thanks when the south winds blow in trials and testings**

B. The garden speaks of fruitfulness.

Galatians 5:22-23 KJV

But the fruit of the Spirit is love, joy, peace, longsuffering, gentleness, goodness, faith,
Meekness, temperance: against such there is no law.

To grow in our relationship with the Lord, to develop trust and faith that these fruit are present in the winds of life; this is true godliness. And when these fruits are manifest in us, another fruit; that of souls coming to be saved, also springs to life through us.

Notice also

C. She is praying for her beloved to come

Which reminds me of:

Titus 2:13 KJV

Looking for that blessed hope, and the glorious appearing of the great God and our Saviour Jesus Christ;

and

2 Timothy 4:8 KJV

Henceforth there is laid up for me a crown of righteousness, which the Lord, the righteous judge, shall give me at that day: and not to me only, but unto all them also that love his appearing.

Living by faith is

- **Praying through the good times and the bad times**
- **Seeking to grow and glorify Him in all of those times and**
- **Looking for and loving His appearing all of the time**

She represents the believers, especially as they are assembled together into a local New Testament Baptist Church (that's the only kind I think there really is). And she is praying. He represents the Lord Jesus Christ and He answers her prayers.

AN ANSWER
Song of Solomon 5:1

Jesus has not come again in the literal sense. We know that He will because He has promised He will. But His presence is with us. When we draw nigh to Him, we sense His nearness even now.

Notice what He says here is all about answers to prayer.

- **I have come**
- **I have gathered**
- **I have eaten**
- **I have drunk**

And then He invites His beloved to eat and drink.

The other day I read the account of Martha being cumbered about much serving again. In effect she is praying to the Lord and it occurred to me that her account teaches us a forth type of answer to prayer.

57

Luke 10:40-42 KJV

But Martha was cumbered about much serving, and came to him, and said, Lord, dost thou not care that my sister hath left me to serve alone? bid her therefore that she help me.

And Jesus answered and said unto her, Martha, Martha, thou art careful and troubled about many things:

But one thing is needful: and Mary hath chosen that good part, which shall not be taken away from her.

We often say that God always answers our prayers and that:

- **Sometimes the answer is yes**
- **Sometimes the answer is no**
- **Sometimes the answer is wait**

The fourth potential answer is:

- **Sometimes, the answer is to correct and change our thoughts, priorities and conclusions on the subject about which we pray.**

And I think maybe that is the most common answer to prayer we have. Very often we think we are praying in the will of God, but as we keep on praying, searching the Scriptures and seeking the Lord's guidance we find out that we are off base.

It is through our prayer that the Lord corrects and molds us and reshapes how we think about the things for which we pray.

Living by faith is:

- **Praying through the north winds and south winds of life**
- **Growing in grace through them and glorifying God in them**
- **Watching for Jesus in the midst of them and**
- **Learning from Jesus as we pray through them**

[1] Chapter 3:6-11
[2] Luke 8:35

Section Five - The Church Age

Chapter 12

LOVER'S SPAT
Song of Solomon 5:1-6

It happens in every relationship: someone gets upset at the other for something. The situation grows worse as each one miscommunicates with the other and pretty soon things are blown way out of proportion. Solomon's song teaches us that such spats happen in the realm of the spiritual relationship too.

The process to spiritual new birth was, as Solomon described it, a gradual and progressive one. The Shulamite, who represents every soul who has an interest in the things of God, has gone from that innate awareness of God to a place of earnest interest in God, to new birth in Christ, to the joys of the early experiences of the believer. There have been some bumps along the way but in the metaphor Solomon is using, they are married.

You know what follows marriage don't you? Married life.
- **Year after year of growing together**
- **Year after year of putting up with each other**
- **Year after year of paying bills, raising children, buying groceries and eating meals**

Valentines Day comes after about 10 or 15 years of this and the wife says, "Honey, I can barely remember life without you." He retorts, "Yes, it seems like forever!"

There is a thing that happens in the spiritual realm where, after a few years of being saved, the newness wears off. Sometimes we forget the blessing it is to be saved. We don't see daily miracles. We find that we are called to be servants and we find out that part of our duties are as soldiers There are hardships.

There are misunderstandings – we didn't know Christianity was going to be just like this.

Three key parts to this passage:
HE IS AWAY
Song of Solomon 5:2 KJV
I sleep, but my heart waketh:

This is the voice of the Shulamite. The idea is that she is at home, she's gone to bed, she is fallen asleep dreaming about her love – but he isn't there. You get the impression that she is expecting him any time. But then He doesn't come. She grows a little restless, then maybe a bit disappointed and perhaps even a bit upset.

We are right there spiritually. When it comes to the doctrine of the coming of the Lord Jesus Christ we have every sort of idea about what might or might not happen. Paul said that Jesus would rapture the Christians to heaven "*In a moment, in the twinkling of an eye.*"[1] Jesus said that it would happen in a moment when ye think not. Again Paul said, "*Then we which are alive and remain shall be caught up together with them in the clouds.*"[2] Paul believed he could be raptured to heaven before the Tribulation and without tasting death. If it could have happened in Paul's day but didn't, it is much more likely to happen now. Jesus is going to come again. It is a day and an hour only God the Father knows and it will happen suddenly and without warning. Christians will be caught up all at the same time into heaven before the Tribulation Period with those saints who are resurrected from the grave. But over the centuries people have gotten tired of waiting. They have developed other doctrines like:
- **Maybe Jesus has already come in a spiritual way**
- **Maybe Jesus isn't coming and it is up to us to set up His kingdom**
- **Maybe He is going to come after the Tribulation or more recently even some Independent Baptists have conjectured**
- **Maybe He is going to come during the Tribulation**

Some just scoff and say, "*Where is the promise of His coming? for since the fathers fell asleep, all things continue as they were*"[3] They misunderstood. They thought He was coming right away and they got into a spat so that…

SHE'S NOT READY WHEN HE KNOCKS
Song of Solomon 5:2-3 KJV
… it is the voice of my beloved that knocketh, saying, Open to me, my sister, my love, my dove, my undefiled: for my head is filled with dew, and my locks with the drops of the night.
I have put off my coat; how shall I put it on? I have washed my feet; how shall I defile them?

The shepherd has been away, probably longer than she thought he would be. Now, when he comes home and knocks on the door of her room, she won't let him in.

Ever gotten that way in your marriage?
- **You thought your spouse would be home at a certain time**
- **When they did not get home right then, you got worried for them but**
- **When they did get home (late), you were upset about it**

Ever been like that spiritually?
- **You thought the Lord would do this certain thing for you**
- **When he did not do it just like you expected, you got disappointed**
- **Then you got disenchanted with the Lord and backslid**

Since Jesus didn't take us to heaven right away, and life began to happen, with all of its tangled up troubles and tricky trials, many Christians not only stop looking for Jesus to come, they stop living like a Christian ought to.

HE DOESN'T HANG AROUND
Song of Solomon 5:5-6 KJV
I rose up to open to my beloved; and my hands dropped with myrrh, and my fingers with sweet smelling myrrh, upon the handles of the lock.
I opened to my beloved; but my beloved had withdrawn himself, and was gone: my soul failed when he spake: I sought him, but I could not find him; I called him, but he gave me no answer.

Be careful not to think of this as representing what happens if a Christian is not ready when Jesus comes again. First of all, it would not be in sync with the story line because there is going to be a bunch more living to be done. Secondly, it would not be accurate theology since one who is saved can never be forsaken of the Lord. The picture here is not of the rapture but of a spiritual closeness to the Lord. While Jesus will never leave or forsake us, there is a joy of our salvation that can be lost whenever a Christian refuses to live in harmony and closeness to the Lord.

Just one "for instance" passage:
1 John 1:6 KJV
If we say that we have fellowship with him, and walk in darkness, we lie, and do not the truth:
This passage is all about Christians and it says three things:
- **A Christian can lie**
- **A Christian can walk in darkness**
- **To do so is to forsake fellowship with Christ**

A Christian can never lose their salvation but they can sure lose the rewards of that salvation – both now and in heaven.

[1] 1 Corinthians 15:52
[2] 1 Thessalonians 4:17
[3] 2 Peter 3:4

Chapter 13

WHAT HAPPENS AFTER A FALL?
Song of Solomon 5:7-9

1. The Song of Solomon is a play.
It is not a historical record but a theatrical representation.
2. The picture in the play is a young couple in love.
But the subject being treated is Christ's love for His church, or in Old Testament times, God's love for Israel.
3. SOS 5:1-6 represents a misunderstanding on the part of the church, the bride.
The marriage has occurred but the groom is gone longer than she expected. She gets crossways with the groom, and their fellowship is broken. She quickly realizes that the distance is there but, as every married person in this room knows, fellowship can take much longer to restore than to break!

There are at least three stages I can find in verses 7-9:
CONVICTION
Vs 7

The watchman is certainly a type for the pastor/preacher.
Hebrews 13:17 KJV
Obey them that have the rule over you, and submit yourselves: for they watch for your souls, as they that must give account, that they may do it with joy, and not with grief: for that is unprofitable for you.

Whenever our relationship with the Lord is not what it ought to be, the words of the preacher can be pretty painful, can't they? Truth be told, you wouldn't really benefit from a preacher who comforted you when your fellowship with Christ is strained.

If he isn't going to:
- **Correct you**
- **Direct you**
- **Motivate you**

Back to the Lord, He is pretty much a waste of your time. But it still hurts.

The question is, how will you respond to the pain?
- **Will you accept it and improve because of it?**
- **Will you reject it, get mad and quit because of it?**

CRYING
Vs 8

There are three phrases in this verse I want to point out:
A. Tell him
The bride is here asking for some help. She is enlisting others to pray for her and to help her as she seeks to restore her fellowship with the Lord. She is crying out to them to cry out to the Lord for her. Christian, take the requests of others for prayer seriously!

B. I am sick of love
She is asking them to pray for her, but she is asking for a very specific prayer request. She is asking them to tell the Lord, she longs for Him.

When you pray for people, pray specifically about their walk with the Lord.
- **They might need money**
- **They might need health**
- **They might have some worldly heartaches**
But none of those is so important as that we walk with the Lord.

C. If ye find my beloved
There were no guarantees that they would find Him. Though it is always best to have others praying for us and with us, the responsibility for our fellowship with and obedience to Christ always falls on ourselves.

The third verse for today's study addresses what I am going to call,

CONFUSION
Vs 9

She asks for help to find Him and those she asks ask back, "What's so special about this guy?" The Bible says of Jesus Christ

Isaiah 53:1-2 KJV

Who hath believed our report? and to whom is the arm of the LORD revealed?

For he shall grow up before him as a tender plant, and as a root out of a dry ground: he hath no form nor comeliness; and when we shall see him, there is no beauty that we should desire him.

I am afraid that, even in good Baptist churches, we have constructed a kind of false Christ.

We have tried to make Christianity look appealing. We talk about Christianity as if when you get saved,

- **Marriages turn out better**
- **Kids grow up better, smarter, and more successful**
- **Jobs automatically promote you**
- **Cars never break**

None of that is necessarily true. Those things can be byproducts of our walk with the Lord, but they don't have to be. Truth be told, the Christ of the Bible did nothing to sell Himself to the general public.

He just went around telling people the truth:

- **That sin would send a man to hell**
- **That religion was broken and not helping them**
- **That faith in Him was the only way to restore fellowship with God and live with Him eternally.**

There are some other subjects that are addressed in the Bible, and they all have their place – but they come in second to all of that.

Verse 9 they ask her, "What's so special about Him?" Verses 10-16 is her reply. That's for another lesson.

Chapter 14

COUNTING THE WAYS
Song of Solomon 5:10-16 KJV
Song of Solomon 6:1-2 KJV

> How do I love thee? Let me count the ways.
> I love thee to the depth and breadth and height
> My soul can reach, when feeling out of sight
> For the ends of Being and ideal Grace.
> I love thee to the level of everday's
> Most quiet need, by sun and candlelight.
> I love thee freely, as men strive for Right.
> I love thee purely, as they turn from Praise.
> I love thee with the passion put to use
> In my old griefs, and with my childhood faith.
> I love thee with a love I seemed to lose
> With my lost saints, - I love thee with the breath,
> Smiles, tears, of all my life! – and, if God choose,
> I shall but love thee better after death.[1]

When we ended the lesson last Sunday morning, it was with a question. The bride had gone to seek her beloved. She had gotten out of sorts with Him and her fellowship has been broken. In her desire to get things right, she has requested help from the daughters of Jerusalem.

Their response is, Song of Solomon 5:9 KJV
What is thy beloved more than another beloved, O thou fairest among women? what is thy beloved more than another beloved, that thou dost so charge us?
"What's so special about this guy?"

And remember, we ended the lesson with Isaiah 53:2 KJV
For he shall grow up before him as a tender plant, and as a root out of a dry ground: he hath no form nor comeliness; and when we shall see him, there is no beauty that we should desire him.
From the earthly point of view, Jesus offers no reason to be attracted to Him.

- **He isn't wealthy**
- **He isn't powerful**
- **He isn't well traveled**
- **He isn't well bred**

If we take Isaiah 53 literally,
- **He wasn't even particularly handsome**

That was all from last week's lesson. This morning I want to point out that there is actually a series of two questions the daughters of Jerusalem asked the bride

1. **What makes Him so special?**[2]
2. **Where is He now?**[3]

ANSWER NUMBER ONE
Song of Solomon 5:10-16

They ask her what is so special about Him. She says, "Just let me count the ways!" One of the most conclusive signs that a person is genuinely born again is this; can they describe Christ's loveliness?

To the lost person Jesus was:
- **A Jewish insurrectionist**
- **A historic figure or maybe even**
- **A fictional character**

To a religious but lost person Jesus was:
- **A good teacher**
- **A great prophet**
- **A spiritual example**
- **An answer to their troubles**
- **A cure for their diseases**
- **An escape from their prison**
But Jesus is so much more than that!

As I have said a number of times, the Song of Solomon is a song, a play, a metaphor for the relationship God has with His people:
- **God and Israel in the Old Testament**

We don't have to try to find a way to make the physical parts described in verses 10-16 symbolize what is beautiful about Jesus. We have an entire New Testament to do that for us! I do notice however, that her description is all about him and not about her connection with him.

I will tell you what is so special about Jesus Christ.

A. His sinless perfection
Hebrews 4:15 KJV

For we have not an high priest which cannot be touched with the feeling of our infirmities; but was in all points tempted like as we are, yet without sin.

B. His wondrous compassion
Matthew 9:36 KJV

But when he saw the multitudes, he was moved with compassion on them, because they fainted, and were scattered abroad, as sheep having no shepherd.

C. His vicarious crucifixion
2 Corinthians 5:21 KJV

For he hath made him to be sin for us, who knew no sin; that we might be made the righteousness of God in him.

D. His measureless justification
John 6:37 KJV

All that the Father giveth me shall come to me; and him that cometh to me I will in no wise cast out.

E. His endless Intercession
Hebrews 7:25 KJV

Wherefore he is able also to save them to the uttermost that come unto God by him, seeing he ever liveth to make intercession for them.

The things that make Jesus "special" more than any other, are all things that can only be appreciated by those who are saved. So that I can know that if a person really appreciates these things about Jesus, they are really saved. If it is anything else, they have a false hope.

ANSWER NUMBER TWO

Song of Solomon 6:1-3 KJV

Whither is thy beloved gone, O thou fairest among women? whither is thy beloved turned aside? that we may seek him with thee.
My beloved is gone down into his garden, to the beds of spices, to feed in the gardens, and to gather lilies.
I am my beloved's, and my beloved is mine: he feedeth among the lilies.

Did you notice the very definite change in the attitude of the daughters of Jerusalem?

Now they are asking her,

- **Where is He?**
- **May we seek Him with thee?**

There is great hope in this passage. It begins with her having lost fellowship with the one she loves but it ends with her bringing others to love Him too. I am reminded of King David's fall with Bathsheba.

Psalms 51:1-5 KJV

To the chief Musician, A Psalm of David, when Nathan the prophet came unto him, after he had gone in to Bathsheba.
Have mercy upon me, O God, according to thy lovingkindness: according unto the multitude of thy tender mercies blot out my transgressions.
Wash me throughly from mine iniquity, and cleanse me from my sin.
For I acknowledge my transgressions: and my sin is ever before me.
Against thee, thee only, have I sinned, and done this evil in thy sight: that thou mightest be justified when thou speakest, and be clear when thou judgest.
Behold, I was shapen in iniquity; and in sin did my mother conceive me.

The King was caught in his sin and despised himself because of it.

- **He said his sin is ever before him – the burden is eating him up**
- **He said his sin is against God and is evil**
- **He said he has been a sinner since he was born**

He's wallowing, smitten in his sin. He then begs for forgiveness and asks God to create a clean heart in him.

And then he says,
Psalms 51:13 KJV
... I teach transgressors thy ways; and sinners shall be converted unto thee.

Far from being ruined forever, God could use him to win sinners to the Lord. There is a revival happening here! *Whither is thy beloved gone, O thou fairest among women?* They are looking at her differently now too. Now she has influence upon them. Now she has the ability lead them to love the one she loves so much. It was not because she had talked about all the things the Lord had given her – she talked about Him.

Her answer:
My beloved is gone down into his garden

I am reminded of another passage:
John 14:2-3 KJV
In my Father's house are many mansions: if it were not so, I would have told you. I go to prepare a place for you.
And if I go and prepare a place for you, I will come again, and receive you unto myself; that where I am, there ye may be also.

That's where He is right now. I know that one day, I believe it will be very soon, He will come again and receive me unto himself. And I want to spend the rest of my life inviting other to come along.

[1] Elizabeth Barrett Browning, Sonnets from the Portuguese, Number 43
[2] Song of Solomon 5:9
[3] Song of Solomon 6:1

Chapter 15

RESULTS OF REVIVAL
Song of Solomon 6:4-13

In order for us to grasp what we have in this passage, I think, is necessary to review the timeline that is presented in the five acts outlined in the Song of Solomon:

1. Initial drawing to the Saviour
1:1-2:7
2. Conviction prior to salvation
2:8-3:5
3. The new Birth
3:6-5:1
4. The Church Age - while He is away
5:2-8:7
5. Heaven, Christ's return
8:8-14

We are deeply into the fourth act of the Song. Our relationship with Christ formally begins at the moment of salvation. For most of us that moment, and the first ones after it, are nearly miraculous, amazing and wonderful. We feel the liberty of our sins being forgiven. We have the hope of our eternal home in Heaven. We believe in the Lord's direction for life from now on.

But, like the bride of the Song of Solomon, we are prone to misunderstand the Lord's full intentions for us and it is not impossible for a Christian to get bent out of shape toward the Lord. We discover that He is in charge of this relationship and not the other way around.

The Shulamite expected her beloved to come home at a particular time.
- **When he did not, she got crossways**
- **In getting crossways, she lost her fellowship with her beloved**

She soon came to her "spiritual senses" and began seeking to restore that relationship and in the process a revival took place.
- **She sought him**
- **She heard a convicting message (or messages) from the watchman**
- **She declared her love for her beloved**

The result of her revived heart was twofold:
- **Others asked to join her in seeking her beloved**
- **Her beloved restored his conversation with her (she found Him)**

What we have in our passage is the restoration of communication between her and her beloved. The entire passage except the final verse is from the Groom, who is a representation of Jesus Christ.

Note these qualities of the Lord's conversation:

IT REPEATS SOME PREVIOUS CONVERSATION
Vs 5-6

Remember that this section began with broken fellowship between her and her beloved. We have seen that once she got things right she was able to influence others to seek Him but it is not until here that she knows things are right between her and her groom.

We have heard these words before:
Song of Solomon 4:1-2 KJV
Behold, thou art fair, my love; behold, thou art fair; thou hast doves' eyes within thy locks: thy hair is as a flock of goats, that appear from mount Gilead.
Thy teeth are like a flock of sheep that are even shorn, which came up from the washing; whereof every one bear twins, and none is barren among them.

The point is that, though the fellowship had been strained for a time, the relationship had not been damaged. He felt the same way about her now as he had before.

IT IS GLOWING WITH PRAISE
Vs 4; 7-10

I am reminded of Ephesians 5:25-27 KJV
Husbands, love your wives, even as Christ also loved the church, and gave himself for it;
That he might sanctify and cleanse it with the washing of water by the word,
That he might present it to himself a glorious church, not having spot, or wrinkle, or any such thing; but that it should be holy and without blemish.

I think that one of the biggest blessings the Christian may possess is the knowledge that God only sees Christ in us.

2 Corinthians 5:21 KJV
For he hath made him to be sin for us, who knew no sin; that we might be made the righteousness of God in him.

Because we are in Christ, when He looks at us, God only sees the righteousness of God.

IT EXPRESSES CHRIST'S CONDESCENSION TOWARD HIS OWN
Vs 5

The commentaries say that this is reminiscent of Jacob's wrestling with God and prevailing. It carries the idea that, as we look to the Lord in love and adoration, yes, but in earnest desire and expectation for our needs, He is overcome with compassion and desire to fulfill our heart's request.

IT ACKNOWLEDGES FRUIT FROM HER
Vs 11

Always expect that God's purpose is fruit, not only fruit on our account but fruit that we have produced. God looks for the fruit. Notice that there are listed:
- **Nuts**
- **Grapes**
- **Pomegranates**

We do not all produce the same fruit or the same quantities; but we should all produce spiritual fruit for the cause of Christ.

IT ATTRACTS THE ATTENTION OF OTHERS
Vs 13

There is an obvious change of voices here from the Beloved Groom, to those daughters of Jerusalem. They request that the Shulamite return in such a way as that they may investigate and look upon her.

Interestingly,
- **When the Shulamite gave praise to her beloved, the Daughters of Jerusalem desired to seek Him**
- **When the beloved groom gave praise toward his bride, the Daughters of Jerusalem longed to know her better**

As we draw ever closer to the Lord, the world around us will be drawn to Christ, and Christ will draw them back to us.
- **The way to win people to Christ and Christianity (our church) is not to be like them and befriend them.**[1]
- **The way to win people around you is to love the Lord your God with all of your heart and your soul and your mind. As you love the Lord, those around you will be drawn to Christ and He in turn will point them back to our churches.**

- **We don't win the world by making them part of our church.**
- **We win the world by making them disciples of Christ. Christ then directs them into Bible preaching churches where they can be baptized and taught to observe all things Christ has commanded.**

I am going to close with a final comment from verse 13. The Daughters of Jerusalem observe that the Shulamite (a representative of the Christian) is like two armies. This is especially appropriate because they have seen her out of fellowship with her beloved and they have witnessed her beloved's love for her. In other words they have seen both her fleshly (sinful) side and her spiritual side.

Romans 7:23 KJV
But I see another law in my members, warring against the law of my mind, and bringing me into captivity to the law of sin which is in my members.

Galatians 5:17 KJV
For the flesh lusteth against the Spirit, and the Spirit against the flesh: and these are contrary the one to the other: so that ye cannot do the things that ye would.

I don't believe it is wrong for you to acknowledge that you have a fleshly side. I just want to advise you not to surrender to it.

[1] I am not recommending we be unfriendly. I am only saying that to befriend the world will never really win the world.

Chapter 16

SWEETER EVERY DAY
Song of Solomon 7:11-13 KJV

A favorite hymn for me to sing is **"Still Sweeter Every Day"**[1]
> *To Jesus every day I find my heart is closer drawn*
> *He's fairer than the glory of the gold and purple dawn*
> *He's all my fancy pictures in its fairest dreams and more*
> *Each day He grows still sweeter than he was the day before*

One of the happiest days of my whole life was the day I became a Christian. And while I cannot say that there have never been any trials, I can say that I have not regretted one second of salvation. Every day with Jesus IS sweeter than the day before.[2]

Chapter seven is obviously a continuation of the last part of chapter six where the shepherd, who represents the Lord Jesus Christ, is expressing his love and adoration for his Shulamite, a representation of the believers. There was a small interruption at the end of chapter six where the daughters of Jerusalem, who represent the onlookers of the relationship[3] ask the Shulamite to give them a chance to get to know her too.

Chapter seven, verses one through nine, takes right back up with the Lord expressing his love for His beloved. It represents, in my mind, our current relationship with Jesus and what is the intent of that relationship.

I am reminded of, Romans 8:28-30 KJV
And we know that all things work together for good to them that love God, to them who are the called according to his purpose.
For whom he did foreknow, he also did predestinate to be conformed to the image of his Son, that he might be the firstborn among many brethren.

76

Moreover whom he did predestinate, them he also called: and whom he called, them he also justified: and whom he justified, them he also glorified.

The Lord is in the business of glorifying you today. In order for that to happen - there has to be some sanctification - there has to be a process of perfection; Ephesians 4:11-13 KJV
And he gave some, apostles; and some, prophets; and some, evangelists; and some, pastors and teachers;
For the perfecting of the saints, for the work of the ministry, for the edifying of the body of Christ:
Till we all come in the unity of the faith, and of the knowledge of the Son of God, unto a perfect man, unto the measure of the stature of the fulness of Christ:

There is your church right there!

Verses one through nine remind me of another New Testament passage; Ephesians 6:13-18 KJV
Wherefore take unto you the whole armour of God, that ye may be able to withstand in the evil day, and having done all, to stand.
Stand therefore, having your loins girt about with truth, and having on the breastplate of righteousness;
And your feet shod with the preparation of the gospel of peace;
Above all, taking the shield of faith, wherewith ye shall be able to quench all the fiery darts of the wicked.
And take the helmet of salvation, and the sword of the Spirit, which is the word of God:
Praying always with all prayer and supplication in the Spirit, and watching thereunto with all perseverance and supplication for all saints;

Both passages give a description that is "head to toe".

Song of Solomon 7:10 KJV has the Shulamite responding,
I am my beloved's, and his desire is toward me.

We could avoid so much worldliness and grow in our faith so much more quickly if we ever got hold of this realization; *the Lord desires us.* He longs for our fellowship, for us to come out of this world and come to Him. Hebrews 13:13 KJV, **Let us go forth therefore unto him without the camp, bearing his reproach.** He yearns to see us walk by faith and not by sight. The Lord is not passive about our relationship with Him. He is:

- **passionate**
- **particular**
- **positioned to welcome us when we step in His direction**

John 6:37 KJV
All that the Father giveth me shall come to me; and him that cometh to me I will in no wise cast out.

SHE SEEKS SEPARATION

Song of Solomon 7:11 KJV
Come, my beloved, let us go forth into the field; let us lodge in the villages.

She wants out of the hustle and bustle of Jerusalem and back to the fields where they met. She wants away from the distractions from their relationship. She wants, as the apostle Paul commanded us, to "*come out of this world and be ye separate.*"[4]

Everyone who loves the Lord and knows that the Lord loves them, strives to become less and less attached to this world.

SHE SEEKS EXAMINATION

Song of Solomon 7:12 KJV
Let us get up early to the vineyards; let us see if the vine flourish, whether the tender grape appear, and the pomegranates bud forth: there will I give thee my loves.

I am reminded again of John 15:1-2 KJV
I am the true vine, and my Father is the husbandman.
Every branch in me that beareth not fruit he taketh away: and every branch that beareth fruit, he purgeth it, that it may bring forth more fruit.

She says to her love, "Let's go see how the fruit is doing."

King David prayed, Psalms 139:23-24 KJV
Search me, O God, and know my heart: try me, and know my thoughts:
And see if there be any wicked way in me, and lead me in the way everlasting.

Do you pray like that? Don't be afraid of what He will find. Welcome it. Let Him purge you from it so that you may be perfected and conformed, not to this world but into the image of Jesus Christ.

SHE SEEKS REPRODUCTION
Song of Solomon 7:13 KJV
The mandrakes give a smell, and at our gates are all manner of pleasant fruits, new and old, which I have laid up for thee, O my beloved.

Remember how Rachel and Leah argued over mandrakes because they believed that they would help them reproduce children? The desire of every Christian ought to be to produce Spiritual fruit:
- **Love**
- **Joy**
- **Peace**
- **Longsuffering**
- **Gentleness**
- **Goodness**
- **Faith**
- **Meekness**
- **Temperance**

And, conversions of lost souls to the Saviour. I do not believe there is any conflict between Christians producing the fruit of the Spirit or the fruit of lost souls being saved. The fruit is both. God wants both. Christians who are thinking right also want both.

[1] Author, William C. Martin
[2] Author, Wendell Loveless
[3] Remember that people are constantly observing and judging those of us who claim to know the Lord. That's not a bad thing. It is how they will come to be drawn to the Saviour themselves.
[4] 2 Corinthians 6:17 KJV
Wherefore come out from among them, and be ye separate, saith the Lord, and touch not the unclean thing; and I will receive you,

Chapter 17

ONE ON ONE
Song of Solomon 8:1-7 KJV

In one of the earliest lessons in this series, I said that some Bible students have pointed out a similarity between the Song of Solomon and the seven churches of Asia in the book of the Revelation of Jesus Christ.

A. Meeting
This parallels with the church at **Ephesus**.
They are in love but they have some problems.

B. Dating
Which parallels perhaps the church at **Smyrna** of which Jesus says they are impoverished but rich.

C. Courting
There is a section in the Song of Solomon where the couple are torn apart by the King, who has abducted her from her shepherd. This could be the church at **Pergamos**, who hold the doctrine of the Nicolatians, which the Lord hates.

D. Wedding
The church at **Thyatira**. Jesus know their works, charity, service, faith, patience and works again.

E. Living - he's gone, she misunderstands
There are only two churches Jesus says nothing good about. **Sardis** is the first of those. She has a name that she lives but she is dead.

F. Reviving
The church of **Philadelphia** is the only one of the seven churches Jesus has nothing against.

Chapter 8:1-7 describe the Shulamite, a picture of Christians – absolutely in love with her beloved, a picture of Jesus Christ.

If in fact the seven churches of Asia describe seven periods of church history, then I think we are already passed the Philadelphia age and we are into the Laodicean period when most Christians are satisfied with themselves and are probably as lost as they can be. However, I am sure that the seven churches of Asia describe seven sorts of "spirits" that individual churches and certainly individual Christians can have. That means that even if we are in a generally Laodicean spirit right now, any individual Christian and any individual church can be a Philadelphian spirit.

G. Retreating
The last church is **Laodicea**, of which Jesus says nothing good. But there is a good thing associated with it. It is just after the Laodicean church that Jesus calls the believers to Heaven.

The Song of Solomon ends with a prediction of the coming Groom.

Song of Solomon 8:1-7 then would describe a Philadelphian type relationship with the Lord.

IT IS INTIMATE
It is admittedly intimate, personal and in many respects embarrassing. There is language in this text that is the most sensual in the whole Song of Solomon. It is not vulgar by any means but it is obvious what it is speaking about. This seems appropriate because the picture that Solomon is using to portray a person's relationship with the Lord is the marriage relationship.

If you will remember an earlier chapter I said, "A preacher by the name of A.L. Newton published a book in 1858, called, *The Song of Solomon Compared with Other Scriptures*. In it he wrote, 'Thus the book is full of Jesus. But it is Jesus in peculiar character.

- He is not seen here as Saviour
- Nor as King
- Nor as High Priest
- Nor as Judge
- Nor as Prophet
- Nor as the Captain of our Salvation
- Nor as the great Shepherd of the sheep
- Nor as the mighty God
- Nor as the King of Kings
- Nor as His people's Surety

- No! It is in a dearer and closer relation than any of these – it is Jesus as our Bridegroom, Jesus in marriage union with His bride, His Church.'[1]

The Song of Solomon is the story of the believer who long's to move from a mere servant of Christ to a lover of Christ. Here is the question – **Can you handle intimacy with Jesus Christ?** Or will you settle to hold him, but at an arm's length? **Will you choose to maintain your awkward**, uneasy walk with the Lord? Or will you decide to take His arm, embrace His affections, and begin to pour out to Him your own? Will you settle to have Jesus as your *Saviour*, *King*, *Shepherd*, *High Priest* and *Captain*? Or will you take Him to be your Bridegroom, the lover of your soul?...

…The point is that people who are in love express that love without shame or embarrassment. The point is to verbally and emotionally express love for Jesus Christ and to expect that same love to be reciprocated."

IT IS PERSONAL

It's the kind of relationship that some people cannot be privy too because they just would not understand.

My wife and I are married and everyone knows it.

- We live together
- We wear wedding rings
- We shop, make large purchases and share our lives together

But we don't talk about the personal details of our relationship.

A Christian relationship ought to have both the public and the more personal aspects of it. Let me tell you – if the only Christianity you practice is what you practice in front of people:

- **Your church**
- **Your family**
- **Your spouse**

Then you are missing out on what Christianity really is.

IT IS PRIVATE

It's the sort of relationship that removes you from the normal crowd of believers – they hinder this sort of walk with the Lord. Remember Jesus' metaphor of the broad path, which many take and the narrow path, which few are on. The closer you become to Christ, the fewer people you will see on that path with you.

I believe one of the reasons why we see so little (as in no genuine) revival today is because we have the wrong idea about what revival is. We want revival to:

- **build our churches**
- **swell our numbers**
- **change our world**

Revival may do all of that – but not before it first gets us alone with God.

I used to travel any reasonable distance to hear Jack Hyles preach. Generally those meetings where he preached were packed out with Christians, a lot of them pastors, from all over the area. Before and after the preaching sessions, these Christians would congregate for fellowship in restaurants and motel lobbies and often stay up almost all night long visiting and enjoying one another's company. Dr. Hyles was always conspicuously absent from any of those times of relaxed fellowship.

One time I heard him say why. I don't remember now if it was spoken in a tone meant to bring rebuke, but it surely did that for me. He said that while we were all gathering together, laughing, fellowshipping and reveling in each other's company, he got alone – just him and God, and did the same. Once he described the various places where in those towns he preached in often, he had picked out a private place in a park or some woods or next to a river or maybe just in a Sunday school room, where he would spend hours, just him and God.

Do what you want to with that, but I am pretty sure that most Christians today could not spend more than a few minutes alone with the Lord. Song of Solomon 8:1-7 describes that one on one experience that every healthy relationship especially with the Lord, has to have,

Chapter 18

WE HAVE A SISTER
Song of Solomon 8:8-9

I am following here a train of thought that compares the Song of Solomon to the seven churches of Asia in Revelation chapters 2-3.

One model of teaching those seven churches is to view them as seven distinctive church ages describing for us the entire history of the church age from beginning to its end at the Tribulation period. If that model holds true, the last two ages are represented by
- **Philadelphia** – a church in revival
- **Laodicea** – a church satisfied with itself

Many preachers believe that the highlight of the Philadelphian age was in the 1950-60's with the revival ending in the early to mid 70's. That means we are in the Laodicean era right now. I agree. I think Song of Solomon 8:1-7 describes high point of the church age – Philadelphia. Therefore Song of Solomon 8:8-9 describes the Laodicean age.

A CHANGE OF VOICE
There is someone else speaking now. The voice of the context has gone from the Shulamite describing her love for her Shepherd husband to a plural – a group.

There are a few ways to interpret this:
- **It could be the Shulamite including herself in with a larger group**
- **It could be those daughters of Jerusalem who have figured into this conversation or two or three chapters now**
- **It could be the Shulamite's brothers who had forced her to work the vineyards earlier in the account**

I am going to take it that this is The Shulamite who has included in her plea some others who have come to believe.

The daughters of Jerusalem had become interested in her beloved, and after hearing from Him, they had also become interested in the Shulamite.

In church terms; the testimony of the believers had brought others to meet the Saviour and, when they came to know Jesus as Saviour, they were drawn to become members of His church. As a whole, they are concerned about someone else.

A CONCERNED DESCRIPTION
Vs 8

Various preachers have taught that the little sister here was
A. The Gentile church
As opposed to the earliest church, which was made up of entirely Jewish converts to Christ.

B. The Catholic church
Which, though having the name of a church is anything but what Christ would have desired of his church.

C. The Laodicean church
Which is the tack I am going to take for this lesson.

The fact that she is a "sister" demands that she is in the same family. The description of her implies that she is immature and thus not "marriageable".

The very obvious lesson is that this is someone who claims Christianity but has no real relationship with Christ. The longer I am a Christian the more prone I am to think this is the case of a great many people in our churches today. So very much of what is modern Christianity is all about the form but very little about the Lord.
- **We have our churches**
- **We have our system**
- **We have our right and our wrong**

This is what we do/this is what we don't do. This is what we accept/this is what we do not accept. More and more I am finding that church members are connected to all of those things without having much of any relationship with the Lord.

- **Their prayer life is weak**
- **Their Bible is untouched**

There is cause for concern for them.

A CONSECRATED DETERMINATION
Vs 9

Did you notice that the Bible doesn't say, "We will denounce our sister and leave her to her own end"? They instead determine to do something to help her. If she has not yet "marriageable" they will try to help her become marry-able.

I think what we see here is a "Philadelphia heart" in the midst of a Laodicean age. I re-read the message to the church of Laodicea this week. I noticed that no-where does Jesus say of that church that she is dead.

- **He says she is lukewarm**
- **He says she is wretched and miserable and poor and blind and naked**

But He does not say she is dead. And because she is not dead, there is hope for her.

In fact, Jesus' letter offers her hope. He counsels her. He tells her how to turn things around.

- **She should buy His gold so she would be rich**
- **She should get His raiment so she would be covered**
- **She should anoint her eyes**
- **She should repent**
- **She should open her door to Christ and then**

she would overcome.

I think the Bible message is that the Laodicean age never does turn around as a whole; but there can always be one or two.

- **There could be whole churches that repent and return to Philadephia. If not churches,**
- **There can be people in those churches who repent and become overcomers**

And because there is hope, even if you and I find ourselves in the middle of the Laodicean age – we have work to do!

- **There is somebody YOU can turn from their apathy toward Christ and His church.**
- **There is someone who is lukewarm whose heart can once again be on fire for God.**

It's just up to you and to me to be busy looking for those whose lives can be turned around and back to Jesus Christ.

Chapter 19

VYING FOR THE VINEYARD
Song of Solomon 8:10-12 KJV

Nearing the very end of the Song of Solomon, there is what I believe is a "contest" for the vineyard. Remember that I determined very early on in this series of lessons that Solomon is the villain rather than the hero of the Song.[1] Verses 10-12 represent what will be the very last thing to happen on this earth before Jesus comes again – Satan's contest to reap his own harvest in the world.

There are two voices speaking here:
- **The Shulamite and**
- **The Shepherd**[2]

You will notice in the passage that the subject of the vineyard is mentioned three times.

I am reminded of Revelation 14:14-20 KJV
And I looked, and behold a white cloud, and upon the cloud one sat like unto the Son of man, having on his head a golden crown, and in his hand a sharp sickle.
And another angel came out of the temple, crying with a loud voice to him that sat on the cloud, Thrust in thy sickle, and reap: for the time is come for thee to reap; for the harvest of the earth is ripe.
And he that sat on the cloud thrust in his sickle on the earth; and the earth was reaped.
And another angel came out of the temple which is in heaven, he also having a sharp sickle.
And another angel came out from the altar, which had power over fire; and cried with a loud cry to him that had the sharp sickle, saying, Thrust in thy sharp sickle, and gather the clusters of the vine of the earth; for her grapes are fully ripe.
And the angel thrust in his sickle into the earth, and gathered the vine of the earth, and cast it into the great winepress of the wrath of God.
And the winepress was trodden without the city, and blood came out of the winepress, even unto the horse bridles, by the space of a thousand and six hundred furlongs.

The harvest that is being referred to is the Tribulation period and both the Lord and the devil want to reap.

SATAN SEEKS HIS HARVEST
Vs11
Solomon had a vineyard...

Solomon, recall, is the villain of this plot.
- **He had attempted to spoil the relationship between the Shulamite and the Shepherd**
- **He had ruined his own relationships in real life**
- **He had nearly destroyed his relationship with God because of it[3]**

Eventually he did come to his senses spiritually when he wrote, Ecclesiastes 12:13 KJV
Let us hear the conclusion of the whole matter: Fear God, and keep his commandments: for this is the whole duty of man.

I have been working throughout this series of lessons on the premise that the Song of Solomon is a dream written by Solomon to portray what a relationship with the Lord *ought to be*, and not what his relationship with the Lord *had been*.

Solomon is the villain, then a representative of Satan in this case. And Satan sees the Tribulation as his own vineyard.
2 Thessalonians 2:3-4 KJV
Let no man deceive you by any means: for that day shall not come, except there come a falling away first, and that man of sin be revealed, the son of perdition;
Who opposeth and exalteth himself above all that is called God, or that is worshipped; so that he as God sitteth in the temple of God, shewing himself that he is God.

The Tribulation period is a time of almost unbridled control of Satan, through his Anti-Christ.

2 Thessalonians 2:6-7 KJV
And now ye know what withholdeth that he might be revealed in his time.
For the mystery of iniquity doth already work: only he who now letteth will let, until he be taken out of the way.

The Apostle Paul said that the "mystery of iniquity" was already at work.

- **It was at work in his day**
- **It is at work still today**

But he said that there is something that withholds and restrains it, that will not let it have its unrestricted will on this world. One day that which withholds the iniquity of the Devil will be *"taken out of the way."*

- **Some people say that it is the Holy Spirit of God[4]**
- **Some people believe it to be the believers in this world[5]**

I believe it is the two in unison because, ever since the day of Pentecost, the Holy Spirit permanently resides in the believers: You cannot remove the Holy Spirit from this world without removing the believers too.

The event the Apostle speaks of is the rapture of the saints to heaven. The Tribulation cannot begin so long as the Christians still abide on this earth any more than

- **God would have destroyed the world by the Flood before Noah and his family were in the ark or**
- **He would have judged Sodom and Gomorrah before Lot and his wife and daughters were outside of city**

SATAN'S GOAL IS INSATIABLE

Song of Solomon 8:11 KJV
… he let out the vineyard unto keepers; every one for the fruit thereof was to bring a thousand pieces of silver.

Song of Solomon 8:12 KJV
…thou, O Solomon, must have a thousand, and those that keep the fruit thereof two hundred.

During the Tribulation period Satan, through the Anti-Christ, *"as God sitteth in the temple of God, shewing himself that he is God."* But he is not satisfied ruling just in Jerusalem. He wants the world. He requires men and women to wear a mark that represents him and any who refuse that mark are persecuted and then executed.

91

Satan thinks this is his vineyard. He believes that he is God and the world belongs to him. But God is at work even in this terrible time so that countless numbers of men and women and children come to a saving knowledge of Christ. The devil cannot be satisfied so long as anyone worships any God other than himself. So that the second half of the Tribulation period is worse than the first.

- **In the first half, God pours out judgment on the earth for denying Christ**
- **In the second, Satan pours out wrath on those who have trusted Christ**[6]

JESUS' HARVEST IS CERTAIN
Song of Solomon 8:12 KJV
My vineyard, which is mine, is before me: ...

See in this phrase is the simple plainness of speech. The Shepherd, who represents Jesus Christ, simply says,

- **My vineyard is mine**
- **My vineyard is before me**

It is as if He is telling the devil that, though he has had control of the kingdoms of this world and has thought himself to be the prince and power of this world,

- **this world and all that is in it**
- **is and always has been Christ's**

And when the Tribulation is over – He just takes what is His.

Years ago a family in Astoria invited Anita and I to go on vacation with them, all expenses paid. This couple loved playing tennis and each day of the vacation wanted to play tennis against Anita and me. Thing was, they were so much better than us that it was no contest really.

- **We went through the motions of a game**
- **We followed all the rules of the game**
- **We were in the place the game was played**

But it really wasn't a game at all – ever. It was a "no contest, contest".

That's what the Tribulation is. There is a contest for the vineyard between Satan and the Lord. But it is a "no contest, contest".

[1] This seems reasonable to me, as Solomon, now having come to his spiritual senses, would likely not have represented himself as a hero. He knew the mistakes he had made in his life and wrote this Song of Solomon, among other reasons, as a means to correct the wrong lessons he had taught by his lifestyle.

[2] Who, at one point in the conversation, turns to Solomon and addresses him. Solomon does not reply.

[3] This is the gist of the book of Ecclesiastes. Praise God he came to his senses by the end of it.

[4] Who reproves the world of sin of righteousness and of judgment

[5] Who are salt and light in this world

[6] All the while God's judgments through natural disasters continue.

Section Six – Heaven/Christ's Return

Chapter 20

MAKE HASTE MY BELOVED
Song of Solomon 8:13-14 KJV

The Song of Solomon ends in a manner similar to how the last book of the Old Testament ends, and how the last book of the New Testament ends – with a promise for the soon coming of the Saviour. [1][2]

The Song of Solomon ends in what I believe is a conversation between the Shulamite, representing the believer, and the Shepherd, representing the Lord. In the context it is the bride, the believer, that cries out this last plea, *"**Make haste, my beloved....**"* This is the prayer and cry of the heart of every earnest believer; that Jesus Christ would make haste:

MAKE HASTE THAT OTHERS HEARKEN TO HIS VOICE
Thou that dwellest in the gardens, the companions hearken to thy voice:

2 Corinthians 6:4-10 KJV
But in all things approving ourselves as the ministers of God, in much patience, in afflictions, in necessities, in distresses,
In stripes, in imprisonments, in tumults, in labours, in watchings, in fastings;
By pureness, by knowledge, by longsuffering, by kindness, by the Holy Ghost, by love unfeigned,
By the word of truth, by the power of God, by the armour of righteousness on the right hand and on the left,
By honour and dishonour, by evil report and good report: as deceivers, and yet true;
As unknown, and yet well known; as dying, and, behold, we live; as chastened, and not killed;
As sorrowful, yet alway rejoicing; as poor, yet making many rich; as having nothing, and yet possessing all things.

Beginning in verse 8 the apostle began this series of oxymorons; opposing concepts that are equally true.

- **Honor/dishonor**
- **Evil report/good report**
- **Deceivers/yet true**
- **Unknown/well known**
- **Dying/we live**
- **Sorrowful/always rejoicing**
- **Poor/making rich**
- **Having nothing/possessing all things**

One of the oxymorons of the Christian life is that we long for Jesus to return, but not until our friends have gotten saved. We can sing the song, "*Wait a little longer please Jesus*" and "*O what a wonderful day it will be, Jesus is coming again!*" in the very same church service and mean them both. So it is that in this final plea of the Shulamite she begs that the campanions would hearken to His voice. It has been a recurring thing beginning way back in chapter 5:8[3] that she has addressed the "daughters of Jerusalem" concerning her beloved. While the conversation has been mostly between the Shulamite and the Shepherd but interjected throughout the conversation are places where she speaks to the daughters of Jerusalem, the shepherds speaks to the daughters of Jerusalem and they speak to both the Shulamite and the shepherd.

That makes perfect sense. We, who are believers, do not and are not supposed to live in a vacuum.

- **We are not of this world but**
- **We are in this world**

- **We are naturally going to rub shoulders with people who are not Christians**
- **We are naturally going to speak to them about our faith**
- **They are naturally going to have questions about it**

We want Jesus to come soon. But we would surely love for more to be saved before He comes.

MAKE HASTE THAT I HEAR OF IT
... cause me to hear it.

Not only does the earnest Christian want others to be saved but we want to be a part of God's plan to see them saved. I am glad that people are getting saved that I will never hear about. I am happy that souls are saved in far away countries through the witness of people I have never heard of. But I don't want it to stop there. I want to have some "hands on" experience with winning souls.

- **I want to personally support some of those missionaries in other countries**
- **I want to pray for, encourage and help my church in its soul winning work**
- **I want to win souls my own self**

I will never forget the very first person Anita and I got to lead to Christ. We had been reading books on witnessing and we had been visiting neighbors and homes in around Hermiston where we lived for several months. One day Bro. Ron Bissonnett[4], a telephone repairman who visited the church we belonged to whenever his route had him in our town, told me about a young couple that lived on a farm just outside of Hermiston. He said they seemed to be interested in the gospel and suggested that if a young couple like Anita and I went to speak with them, we might be able to win them to the Lord.

Anita and I went to the house, I knocked on the door and they answered. I went through the plan of salvation with them, and to our delight, they asked the Lord to forgive their sins and save them. When we were finished Anita and I got in our car and drove back home – maybe a 30 minute drive – without saying a word. We had no idea what to say after what we had just experienced.

An earnest Christian wants to be a part of that.

MAKE HASTE TO COME AGAIN
Make haste, my beloved, and be thou like to a roe or to a young hart upon the mountains of spices.

The roe and the hart are types of deer – known for their swiftness.

- **The hope of the Christian is not that we will have a world revival and not that our governments will become better.**
- **The hope of the Christian is not for the right man to be elected next time.**

- **The hope of the Christian is for Jesus Christ to come again.**

- **Until that day we are to work for the Lord.**
- **Until that day we are to watch for the Lord.**

But that day is the day of hope for the saint of God.

[1] Malachi 4:2 KJV
But unto you that fear my name shall the Sun of righteousness arise with healing in his wings; and ye shall go forth, and grow up as calves of the stall.
[2] Revelation 22:20 KJV
He which testifieth these things saith, Surely I come quickly. Amen. Even so, come, Lord Jesus.
[3] That place in the Song where the picture begins to be about the church age.
[4] Bro. Bissonnett later became pastor of the Bible Baptist Church in Burns, OR and later still in Fossil, OR. I do not know the name of that church.

Afterwords

I have represented the Song of Solomon as a play or drama. With that in mind, I want to finish with this brief story from the American Revolution.

After Lord Cornwallis surrendered his army in Yorktown, The Marquis De Lafayette wrote home to simply say, "The play is over."

And so, we finish the Song of Solomon. "The play is over."